CAMBRIDGE LIBRARY COLLECTION

Books of enduring scholarly value

History

The books reissued in this series include accounts of historical events and movements by eye-witnesses and contemporaries, as well as landmark studies that assembled significant source materials or developed new historiographical methods. The series includes work in social, political and military history on a wide range of periods and regions, giving modern scholars ready access to influential publications of the past.

Letters from the Havana, During the Year 1820

Robert Francis Jameson (fl.1820) was the British Commissioner of Arbitration stationed in Cuba between 1819 and 1823. This volume, first published in 1821, contains his observations of Cuba, recorded during his year-long stay in Havana in 1820. Jameson provides a comprehensive description of Cuban society and a detailed account of the city of Havana, illustrating the stark differences between the classes in Havana society. At this time, Cuba was the world's leading producer of sugar cane, and totally dependent on slave labour and the slave trade. Jameson discusses the impact of slavery on the Cuban economy and the advantages and disadvantages of emancipation. He also discusses Cuba's constitutional history and contemporary economy, exploring the effects of Ferdinand VII's opening of Havana to foreign trade. Written in the form of letters to an anonymous recipient, this volume provides a valuable and fascinating picture of contemporary Cuban society.

Cambridge University Press has long been a pioneer in the reissuing of out-of-print titles from its own backlist, producing digital reprints of books that are still sought after by scholars and students but could not be reprinted economically using traditional technology. The Cambridge Library Collection extends this activity to a wider range of books which are still of importance to researchers and professionals, either for the source material they contain, or as landmarks in the history of their academic discipline.

Drawing from the world-renowned collections in the Cambridge University Library, and guided by the advice of experts in each subject area, Cambridge University Press is using state-of-the-art scanning machines in its own Printing House to capture the content of each book selected for inclusion. The files are processed to give a consistently clear, crisp image, and the books finished to the high quality standard for which the Press is recognised around the world. The latest print-on-demand technology ensures that the books will remain available indefinitely, and that orders for single or multiple copies can quickly be supplied.

The Cambridge Library Collection will bring back to life books of enduring scholarly value (including out-of-copyright works originally issued by other publishers) across a wide range of disciplines in the humanities and social sciences and in science and technology.

Letters
from the Havana,
During the Year 1820

*Containing an Account of the
Present State of the Island of Cuba, and
Observations on the Slave Trade*

ROBERT FRANCIS JAMESON

CAMBRIDGE
UNIVERSITY PRESS

CAMBRIDGE UNIVERSITY PRESS

Cambridge, New York, Melbourne, Madrid, Cape Town, Singapore,
São Paolo, Delhi, Dubai, Tokyo, Mexico City

Published in the United States of America by Cambridge University Press, New York

www.cambridge.org
Information on this title: www.cambridge.org/9781108024402

This edition first published 1821
This digitally printed version 2010

ISBN 978-1-108-02440-2 Paperback

REFERENCES TO THE MAP

1. Guanabacoa.
2. Corral falso.
3. Puente blanca.
4. Craz de Santafè.
5. Posada de Vaguraiabo.
6. Ingenio de Pedroso.
7. Guanabo.
8. Ingenio Penal altas de Santa Cruz
9. Ditto San Francisco de Guantanilla
10. Potrero de Giguiabo.
11. Ingenio de Giguiabo.
13. Ditto de Jauregui
14. Ditto Rioblanco de Penalver.
15. Caffetal de Condé de Lorto.
16. Pueblo de Rio blanco.
17. Partido de Santa Cruz.
18. Ingenio de Chavarrias.
19. Ditto de Oviedo.
20. Ditto de Romero.
21. Pueblo de Gibacoa.
22. Partido de Gibacoa.
23. Villa de Santa Maria de Rosario.
24. Ingenio de Alvero.
25. Ditto de S. Josè de Calvo.
26. Potrero de la Savanilla de Casa Bayona.
27. Ingenio La concordia de O'Farrill
28. Pueblo de Taparte.
29. Sierra de la Escalera.
30. La Loma de Cansavacas.
31. Pueblo de S. Juan de Jaruco.
32. Posada de la Diferencia.

33. Iglesia de San Antonio de Pueblo Nuevo.
34. Ditto de San Pablo de Caravallo
35. S. Carlos de Matanzas.
36. Ingenio de San Rafæl de Lanza
37. Ditto de Prado Amens.
38. }
39. } Caffetales
40. Ingenio de Dª· Felicia de Herrera.
41. Caffetal.
42. Igenio Tivitibo de Montalvo
43. Da Trinidad de Penalver
44. S. Miguel de Urnarte.
45. Sª· Ana. de Risel.
46. Megana de Urnarte.
47. La Soledad de Aroztegui.
48. De Garro
49. Galafate de Echegayen
50 La Soledad de Jauregui
51. La Guicanama de Molegon.
52. S. Miguel del Padron o'Potosi
53. Fort Coxèmar.

[Here the English landed in 1762, marching by Guanabacoa to invest Fort Moro.]

54. Fort Moro.
55. Fort Punta.
56. La Cabana. [A battery of 12 guns]
57. El Principe.
58. The Alameda and La Salud.

Ingenios. (bracket spanning 42–51)

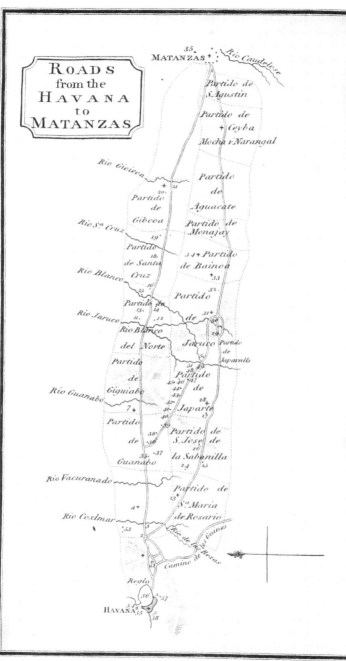

ROADS
from the
HAVANA
to
MATANZAS

MATANZAS

Rio Caudelosa

Partido de S. Agustin

Partido de Ceyba

Mocha v Narangal

Rio Gioicoa

Partido de Gibcoa

Partido de Aguacate

Rio S.ª Cruz

Partido de Monajay

Partido de Santa Cruz

Partido de Bainoa

Rio Blanco

Partido de Jaruco

Rio Jaruco

Partido de

Rio Blanco del Norte

Jaruco

Partido de Japarnils

Partido de Giguiabo

Partido de Japarte

Rio Guanabo

Partido de Guanabo

Partido de S. Jose de la Sabanilla

Rio Vacuranado

Partido de S.ª Maria de Rosario

Rio Coximar

Rio de las Guines

Camino de las Pozas

Regla

HAVANA

LETTERS

FROM

THE HAVANA,

DURING THE YEAR 1820;

CONTAINING-AN ACCOUNT

of the

PRESENT STATE

of

The Island of Cuba,

and

OBSERVATIONS

on

THE SLAVE TRADE.

London:

PRINTED FOR JOHN MILLER, 69, FLEET STREET.

1821.

W. Molineux, Printer, Bream's Buildings,
Chancery Lane.

PREFACE.

THE following Letters contain the results of observation during a year's residence in the island of Cuba. It is by inspection only that the real nature and properties of things can be ascertained, the *notabilia* of Cuba more particularly so, there not being any works that treat of those subjects. Since the affairs of this island have become of sufficient importance to be enquired into, darkness and difficulties have attended research, and it is much easier to give an account of the state of Cuba for the first century of its colonization than to detail it during the last. But it is (to the purposes of useful knowledge) of little consequence to narrate the history of Cuba during the three centuries that elapsed after that event, when the island, though known, was nearly unserviceable to Europe. It is sufficient to learn the causes of that nugatory state and the tardiness of advance exhibited by an island which is by far the finest in the western Archipelago. The philosopher and the politician when they are informed, that a country has been labouring under the desiccating influence of *monopoly* and *restriction* for nearly three centuries, will affirm that it must necessarily, be imperfectly cultivated, thinly peopled, and slenderly provided with capital.

It is from the year 1778 (when one end of the chain which girt the island was loosened and commerce allowed to go the length of its links) that the history of Cuba essentially begins : the narrative of its infancy can only interest its natural relatives. Since the above mentioned year the germs of prosperity, with which it abounds, have begun to vegetate, but during the last eleven years the harvest has been ripening. Since that period the principal ports of the island have enjoyed a free commerce, and the effects of this the following details will exemplify.

The paucity of materials from which regular statements can be made and the mode of acquiring information in the dearth of documents, almost precluded systematic arrangement, but connection has been attempted by digesting the letters into a series.

No apology is offered for giving these details to the public. By the publication of local enquiries the world becomes generally acquainted, and the more intimate mankind is, the better. These are letters of introduction by which the *Cubanas* will be made known to those Englishmen who choose it. I have described them as I saw them. *Chacun a ses lunettes* —mine are *English.*

Havana, October, 1820.

CONTENTS.

———

LETTERS FROM THE HAVANA,

DURING THE YEAR 1820.

LETTER I.

Introduction. Coast and Country of Cuba. West India Society. Population of Cuba; its component parts; stationary nature; character; grades of rank; nobility; *employés;* merchants; clerks; shopkeepers; *montèro's;* people of colour. Amount of *white* population; amount of *coloured* population.

MY DEAR L * * * *

You want a picture of this part of the *new world*, and from *me*, who, I fear, will prove as indifferent a painter as the *old* could furnish. I am inclined, however, to try my *Indian ink* on the subject, for it is, in truth, a fine one—so many striking combinations, stupendous objects and brilliant hues, that a young artist would be completely at home, might draw boldly and colour highly.

A

Insular America has not been much *rummaged* by professional travellers. The yellow demon of fever, with huge red eyes, glares so terrifically at them, that they drop their portfolios in affright. Besides, this is not a climate where a traveller in the writing line can use his seven-league-boots, and, consequently, cannot whisk out quartos with sufficiently profitable rapidity. As a resident, therefore, I possess advantages which I shall avail myself of in giving you some account of this island, the finest in the Western Archipelago.

Nature has robed this portion of the globe with a magnificence and luxuriance far above what our northern regions can boast of. She has bestowed "a coat of many colours" upon this younger world, and plumed it out in all the gaudiness of favored infancy. Perpetual verdure, majestic growth and brilliant colouring, distinguish the vegetable kingdom here—a *kingdom* indeed, full of grandeur, luxury and stateliness, at the head of which stands the *palma real,* or *royal palm**** (whose branches have become the insignia of glory) towering above a long train of noble trees, at whose feet lie thousands of plants drest in the gaudy "livery of the sun." The

---

* Our romantic countrymen at Jamaica call it the "mountain *cabbage!*" In favourable situations it rises nearly 200 feet.

sober truth, in plain language is, that the first
sight of West India scenery is extremely striking,
as much from the grand scale of its creation as
from its perfect novelty to an European eye.
The coasts of the islands are generally low, rising
a short distance from the shore into eminences
covered with palm, coco, tamarind, or orange
trees. I do not know a more elegant tree than
the *palma real.* Its trunk rises to a prodigious
heighth, grey, polished, and tapering, having at
the top a tuft of foliage like a plume of ostrich
feathers. The *coco* is very similar, except that
it is less stately and has its foliage more spread
and depressed. The tamarind is like the elm in
appearance, and in the season of its fruiting, is
covered with small brown pods shaped liked
pears. Of the orange I need scarce speak, except
to desire your imagination to figure the sickly
shoot in a hot-house flower-pot rising into height
and spreading its dark but fresh looking verdure
around the golden fruit with which it is thickly
studded. These are the most common trees to
be found here, and which, with the *papaya* and
aloe (the one with huge upright leaves like drawn
sabres, the other with broad foliage like shields)
are ranked round the patriarchal families of naked
children, pigs, dogs, mules, cats and poultry,

which swarm in the low white huts, covered with thatch that are sprinkled over the hills.

On approaching the shore of Cuba from the north, distance gives a clustered effect to the trees, which, in reality, they do not possess. The country round the Havana is rather bare of them, as might be supposed from its soil being more valuably employed. But the sugar *ingenios* (plantations) which formerly surrounded the city, have now disappeared : the soil has been exhausted, and instead of laboring at its renovation, the planters have gradually receded into the interior, successively occupying new lands, under which class more than half the island may be comprised. This gives rather a forsaken air to the country. Here and there is seen a solitary hut and a patch of maize or plantain ground ; the *palm* lords it over the rest of the scene in lonely grandeur. In all parts of the island this half cultivation is observable. That family intercourse of nature with her children, which is so peculiarly interesting in the well-worked fields of England, is wanting here. Nature produces so bountifully and spontaneously most of the necessaries of life, that man grows indolent. In our northern clime, if nature is less able to act in the service of man, she has more aid from him in proportion to her

weakness and decrepitude. She shares also in
the produce of treasure. We " give her of the
fruit of her hands—her own works praise her."
Palaces, or what are far better, farm buildings and
abodes of utility and comfort, are raised on the
soil, whose harvests have afforded the riches they
evidence—at once altars and testimonies to the
beneficence of nature. Man lives as with a parent
who has done her utmost to serve him, and requites
her efforts by his care : while here he stalks forth
to forage the harvest, drags the spoils of nature
into his pestiferous den, and leaves her to recover
herself as she can.

Though I have scarcely commenced my account
of the Island, I have given you the character of its
vegetation and its people, the one possessed of
surprising energy, the other greatly wanting it.
Perhaps before I begin detailing *things*, it would
be better to take a review of *those* that use them.
I do not propose in my details to stand much on
" the order of my going," but it is the course of
natural history first to describe the animal, then
its den, prey, &c.—I will do the same.

In the description of all countries an account
of the natives forms a principal subject of interest,
but there is a distinctive singularity in the islands
of the new world, called the *West Indies*, that
obliges their historian to be concise on that head,

and to despatch such portion of his history in
these few but comprehensive words—*the natives
are extinct.* Out of an indigenous population consisting of above 3,000,000, who were spread over
these islands, not one remains.* The causes of
this catastrophe are too well and too generally
known to allow of repetition : there is nothing of
novelty to throw into the detail, except it be an
expression of horror at the ravages which the
pestilential fever of avarice has made amongst so
large a portion of our fellow creatures. Dwelling on the graves of this wretched race, are seen
a people of most motley description, collected
from nearly all the nations of the old world,
drawn together by commercial enterprise, speculative cupidity, or the spirit of adventure; amongst
whom appears a numerous progeny of beings,
shaped like men, but who are bought, sold, tram-
pled on and despised as the veriest brutes I could
name. This mass of beings is forcibly conjoined
—their bond of union is a *real chain.* *Fear,* say
the metaphysicians, first formed society, and it is
undoubted that such is the elemental principle of
West India society. Every house is a sort of

---

* The *Black Charaibs* of *Ratan* are descendants of a cargo
of negroes shipwrecked on the island of St. Vincent's, and trans-
ferred from thence by capitulation in 1796 to the first named
place.

garrison filled with domestic conscripts serving without pay and whom it is necessary to guard strictly. In the *ingenio's* or plantations, regiments (to carry on the allusion) of these *pressed men*, are stationed with a proportion of two or three whites to a hundred blacks. The physical disproportion in such situations, (and, generally, in all the islands except *Cuba)* is endeavoured to be remedied by the depression of the moral faculties of the majority, and by severe enactments against their acquiring factitious force. The black man is not allowed to carry any sort of weapon. He dare not venture abroad after night-fall without having a lighted lanthorn in his hand, which marks him out to the white passenger in the same way that a beacon does a point of danger. On the other hand the white man seldom stirs a league from his dwelling without a sword by his side or pistols in his holster ; he breathes round himself a *halo* that magnifies his strength and hides his weakness ; and, to add to his security, clusters himself with his fellows in large bodies notwithstanding the pestilential consequence of such union under a vertical sun.

To be more particular, the component parts of West India population consist of *Europeans ;* of their *legitimate* descendants or *white Creoles ;* of their illegitimate descendants, or *coloured Creoles ;*

and, lastly, of *negroes* who are either *Creoles* or native *Africans*.* In the island of *Cuba* the white classes are a very different description of persons from those usually found in the islands of other nations. In those belonging to England, few proprietors reside. What profits may arise from their estates are expended in Europe, to which, even those who are resident, look as their retreat and place of enjoyment. In Cuba, on the contrary, the *Hacendado's*, or great proprietors, are, almost generally, natives of the island; their ancestors were born there; it is their *country*, in the full sense of the word, in which they live and in which they hope to die. The circumstance of there being *twenty-nine* resident nobility,† many of whom never saw Spain, will show how much more domiciliated the proprietary is here than in our islands. Amongst these and the higher order of planters, are to be found the descendants of the heroes of the sixteenth century, whose names are identified with the glory of Spain. Fixed on the scene of their enterprize, these descendants

---

* These last are called *Bozales*. *Caballo bozal* is a horse not *broken in!* But the term attaches to the native Africans long after they have lost their natural spirit.

† Termed *Titulos de Castilla*, viz. 13 Marquesses and 16 Counts. They pay 9103 dollars annually to the Government under a duty called "*Lanzas*," being a commutation for military service.

have peopled the solitude their fathers made, and
the effect of this stability has been to create a
more numerous *white* population in this *one* island
than in *all the others* of this Archipelago. The
wealth of the island is in the hands of the *Creoles;*
the Europeans being chiefly adventurers from the
north of Spain, with a considerable number of
French, and to this class of whites may be added,
adventurers from the Canaries, from North
America, and the Costa Firme, whose first exertions are commercial, and whose capitals, when
attained, are usually expended in forming plantations. Stakes like these in a country are not easily
plucked up and removed. The adventurer becomes a resident, forms local alliances, and his
children are *cubano's*. This rooting of adventitious
population is, however, as I am inclined to think,
to be chiefly ascribed to the political state of the
mother country, which, with a short interval, has
preserved those feudal distinctions and institutions of the darker ages, which kept society banded
in ranks that none could move from. The
Catalan, the *Gallego*, or other adventurer, when
sent forth to seek his fortune on this shore, knew
that, on attaining the object of his pursuit, his
wealth would scarcely advance him a step in the
scale of society at home. There was no competing
with the lord of his village or the *hidalgos* of his

province—no emparking himself out of some private jurisdiction as an independent *'squire*. On the contrary, in his adopted country his wealth was every day encreasing and raising his importance. If he was ambitious, he could purchase some post of power and distinction in the municipal government of the colony; at any rate he could vie with the greatest in the number of his slaves, and the luxury of his table, and sit down amply satisfied with his own importance.

The *nucleus* of population once formed, a new country afforded a range and facility for its spreading. But though the island of Cuba has been settled above 300 years, it is yet a new country. Shut up during the greatest part of that period by the false policy of Spain, it labored under all the disadvantages of such seclusion, and now shows the effects, by the absence of many useful arts and appendages of refinement long familiar to Europe, as well as by the scanty portion of its soil that lies under cultivation. It is to this we must ascribe, perhaps, the *vis inertiæ* of the *Cubano's* and the small product afforded by the agriculture of an island of such extent. The stimulus of competition was wanting, and where there was natural indolence it met with a fostering system. Thus it happens, that not half the island is cultivated, while half its white population are lounging about with çigars in their mouths, and canes under their arms ;* though like *Gil Blas'* master, *Don Bernardo de Castelblanco*, they are " without lands or rents." Overgrown youths are seen, in social indolence, hanging, like ripe fruit, round the parent stem, which has scarce strength enough to nurture them.

In the *United States* (which being near at hand, form a ready example) the great aim is employment. When every means of local employ is tried, the disappointed endeavourer strikes inland or coastways, and becomes one of the founders of a new mart or a new state. There is no cessation of effort till nature or accumulated misfortunes stop their industry. Here, on the contrary, no one is disposed to *strike out.* The stream of industry and trade struggles through the obstructions of habits and manners with difficulty, running through an aqueduct bed, raised by the enterprizing adventurers of Northern Spain or America. It is sufficient to the creole *caballero* that his country is rich in the germs of prosperity : it is a topic of pride and national exaltation that serves for the discussion of his heavy hours, and he calmly looks down on the enterprising stranger, who is fostering the

---

* A gold or silver-headed cane is one of the exterior insignia of Spanish gentility.

bud and will gather the fruit, as if he were a labourer in his service. This sluggish indifference is chiefly observable in that class amongst whom you would least expect it, viz. those whose means are slender and need improving. As you ascend in society, the view is somewhat brighter. You find men of intelligence and education *awake* to the interests of their country, but they sit in their studies with their *night-caps* on. A profusion of *aviso's, proclama's, manifiesto's,* and *memoria's* are constantly appearing, upon subjects of public benefit, with multitudes of spirited *instigations,* which these gentlemen write in their *arm-chairs* to their neighbours. Now and then one *rises up* to exemplify a project : but the spirit of enterprize is not readily excited ; a quiescent gaze is the only mark of interest, and the attention is then turned to new dissertations on similar subjects.

From what I have said, you may judge of the *tone* of society here amongst the whites. With the highest class, who do not stand in need of exertion, you may conceive that *social ease* is entirely attended to ; that their time is spent in luxurious passiveness ; sometimes broken in on by the love of place ; sometimes agitated by the vacillations of gaming, and sometimes rendered *piquant* by *gallanting* with literature. Almost every one, indeed, *versifies* here, and with the aid of the gods and goddesses, the roses and lilies of Europe, and an assortment of diamonds and gold, odes and sonnets are plentifully manufactured. Something on this subject I may possibly add at another time; suffice it now to say, that " the ample page" of knowledge having been sadly torn in squeezing through the gates of the *Inquisition,* only a few fragments are to be found here.

There are many in the island possessed of very large and numerous estates, but colonial income is precarious, and the expences of living extremely high at the *Havana.* Few, I believe, notwithstanding the high saleable value of their estates can be called *monied* men. Amongst the merchants, large fortunes have been realized, principally by the *slave trade.* But the commercial body, though of primary importance to the island, is only third in rank. The nobility and heads of government departments stand first. The *employés* (of whom I could show you a list of 800) rank second. The merchants, with bags full of gold ounces, march next, followed by a train of Gaditanian French, English, North American and German clerks. Canary Islanders, Biscayners, Gallego's, Catalonians and Americans are the last in order ; but I must not figure them in procession, for they cannot leave their

ground floors and nooks of shops, at the corner
of the great houses, for fear the half-naked black
slave that is piling up their goods should run off
with them; they wisely remain at home, stretched
full length on their counters, dozing between
customers.

There is yet another class of *whites* whom I
have to mention, the *Montero's* or country people,
holders of *estancia's* or small farms, a hardy race,
habituated to exertions, and whose situation
holds out every inducement to make them. Possessed of a few *caballeria's* of land,* on which is a
hut built of flint stones and thatched with the
leaves of the *palma real*, this colonial freeholder
dwells in a sort of patriarchal solitude with his
family, probably ten or twenty miles from a
market. Here he raises maiz, breeds poultry and
pigs, makes charcoal, prepares the thatch called
guano and *yagua* from the leaves and upper rind
of the *palm*, grows vegetables, and gathers in their
season the numerous fruits which nature has
lavishly planted around him. All these various
sources of profit are derived from little comparative labour to what our climate would demand:
but this labour the *Cubano* himself performs,
ploughs, sows, reaps, and conveys the produce to

* A *caballeria* is equal to 32½ acres.

the distant market, which, probably, is the most toilsome portion of his work. Sometimes he is aided by a slave, but very frequently is not able to attain this costly assistance, himself driving his oxen and cropping his field. Having attained temporary wealth, he now seems to consider himself entitled to the privileged indolence of his superiors. He lives careless of the future till his last *real* is about to disappear, and then sets to work again, making, probably, some article of furniture or stock, if his locality will allow of its sale, the means of providing what he may require for support beyond the produce of his *platanar* (plantain grove) or hen roost.

In this class also, I would rank the journeymen carpenters, masons, &c. who are employed at the *ingenio's* and country stations; but their condition and manners assimilate so nearly to those of the free people of colour, with whom they mingle in perfect fellowship, that I shall not particularize them. Indeed, there would seem to be a considerable oozing of *black blood* amongst these *montero's ;* something deeper than the tinge of sunshine on their skins indicates this. Many of them show an *Indian* cross, with long raven-black hair, and full dark eyes set in wrinkles. In others the short curl of hair and flat nose are very "questionable shapes." Others, on the contrary, (and these frequently the poorest and lowest) with bold arched faces half whiskered over, and keen full eyes staring under enormous slouched hats, seem the genuine progeny of the sturdy conquerors of the island. For my part, I view with pleasure this genealogical confusion, surmising a period when slavery, no longer supplied with *African* victims, shall be seen only as the badge of crime, and the population of this noble island, becoming in every sense a *community*, no *colour* shall be considered disgraceful, but the blush that reddens the cheek of foiled tyranny and rentless avarice!

I have thus given you a rapid and slight sketch of the degrees and characteristic of the *white* population. According to the census of 1817, it amounts to 238,796, of whom 129,656 are males, and 109,140 females. A suppository calculation made in *June* 1820 by the Junta Provisional, states its amount at about 320,000, accounting for the very great difference by the influx of foreigners and Spaniards, and the concealment presumed in the authorized census of 1817, from an idea that it was made for the purpose of taxation. I do not entirely agree to these reasons. Whatever influx of Europeans there

might have been,* it is lamentably certain that
25 per cent must be deducted for the loss from
the diseases of the climate ; and, as to the effect
of concealment on the statements rendered under
the census, the government was then too arbitrary and the population too minutely and slenderly spread to admit of evasion. The island
being divided first into *provinces ;* then into
partido's, each from one to two leagues square ;
these into *parroguia's,* affords a full facility to
inspection, and the scrupulous anxiety which a
catholic population evinces not to omit the rites
prescribed by the church, gives the baptisms, mar-
riages and deaths, the three chief statistical data,
with the most perfect fidelity. For these reasons
I am inclined to think that the white population
of Cuba cannot at this time (1820) be stated
higher than 250,000, even allowing for the influx
of emigration and natural increase. The progress of the last may be judged of from the circumstance that, out of 77,821 souls included in
the city and municipal range of the *Havana,*
4015 infants were baptized in 1819, of whom
1302 died, leaving a natural increase of 2713 on

* In the last year (1819) the number of emigrants that arrived
from various countries to reside in the island, amounted to 1332
men, 143 women, and 227 children—total 1702. Of these 201
were from England and Ireland ; 384 from France, and 416 *only
from Spain !*

the total of souls, or about $3\frac{1}{2}$ per cent. During the same period 3891 adults died, or 5 per cent. upon the total; of these 1217 (chiefly European soldiers and sailors) died in hospitals of the epidemic of the country besides many new comers of the same in private houses, leaving, probably, about 2 or $2\frac{1}{2}$ per cent. mortality amongst the creole adults. Taking it thus I do not conceive my statement is very erroneous.

The coloured population of the island (including mulatto and black, bond and free) amounted in 1817 to 314,202 being an excess over the whites of 75,406. Of this number 30,512 were *free mulattoes* and 28,373 *free blacks.* The remaining 124,324 were slaves, consisting of 17,803 mulattoes and 106,521 blacks. To this last number must be added the importation of the three last years, being 25,976 in the year 1817;—about 17,000 in 1818; and 14,668 in 1819, making a total of 181,968 slaves, and an excess of 143,050 over the white population.

The character and condition of this unfortunate race are subjects too important to be discussed in this postscript part of my letter. I must endeavour to do them *justice:* God knows they have no chance of gaining *that* but by the pens and exertions of Englishmen.

I am, &c.

LETTER II.

Slavery; habitual effects of its usage. Coloured population;
    preserve their African character; their nationality; debased
    condition. Efforts of England in the cause of *abolition.*
    Treaties with Spain, Portugal, Netherlands. Mixed Commis-
    sions. Summary of the Spanish Slave Trade. *Free* people
    of colour; their character; number; to what attributable.
    Slaves; domestics; field labourers; difference of their con-
    ditions. Spanish Slave Code; its mildness.

THE European farmer finds that the best
manure is composed of the most offensive materials;—so does the West India planter—he
spreads his fields with orphans and captives, and
expects to find his harvests properous in proportion to the mass of misery he has heaped together.
This assertion will show you that I have not yet
suffered that *ossification of the heart* which a residence in the West Indies too often occasions.
Habit, they say, is a second nature : our *primary*
nature is bad enough, and when the two are conjoined, strange anomalies are produced. Thus you

B 2

may meet here with many *honourable slave dealers*
and *liberal minded slave owners*. I am not sufficiently acclimated in my feelings to rank under
either character; slaves I have none, my household is composed partly of Europeans, partly of
free blacks, and notwithstanding the considerably
higher expence of such arrangement, I find myself much better off than my neighbours.

The *coloured* population in all the islands form
the majority, and though thrown out of the ranks
of society, impress on it a character more or less
peculiar according to their number or their usuage.
In none of the islands do they appear to have ac-
quired an indigenous character; the African soil,
from which they were torn, still clings to them,
neither washed off in the font of baptism or the
stream of knowledge. As to the last, indeed, it
purls round without touching them; they are
carefully restricted from any acquirements incon-
sistent with their state of degradation, for the
value of the *slave* is raised in proportion as the
qualities of the *man* are destroyed. In Europe
they *blind* mill-horses to make them work better—
they pluck the *head* off the bean to make it bear
more fully; these and other *improvements upon
nature* the West India planter has not forgotten.

It is true that the negro is taught the ritual of
religion—(and religion here is a ritual only)—

strongly and practically lessoned to despise this world and look forward with hope to a better; but his *fetiche* is only laid aside for a *relique*—(so far there is a *change* in his religion)—the barbarism of superstition remains—the mist is not removed from his intellect—it is but agitated by the intrusion of new ideas and soon settles thickly around them. That he should preserve, even after the lapse of generations, all the features of his former state, is not to be wondered at. Little is done to remove them; they are, as it were, but partially hid under his new habits. The different nations to which the negroes belonged in Africa are marked out in the colonies both by the master and the slave; the former considering them variously characterized in the desired qualities, and the latter joining together with a true national spirit in such union as their lords allow. Each tribe or people has a *king* elected out of their number, whom, if they cannot enthrone in *Ashantee* glory, yet they *rag* out with much savage grandeur on the holidays in which they are permitted to meet. At these courtly festivals (usually held every Sunday and feast day) numbers of free and enslaved negroes assemble to do homage with a sort of grave merriment that one would doubt whether it was done in ridicule or memory of their former condition. The *gong-gong*—

(christianized by the name of *diablito*), *cows-horns*, and every kind of inharmonious instrument, are florished on by a gasping band, assisted by clapping of hands, howling and the striking of every sounding material within reach, while the whole assemblage dance with maniac eagerness till their strength fails. The only *civilized* part of the entertainment is—*drinking rum*.

But I know not to what purpose I should detail circumstances of this kind. So much has been published about *Africa*, of late, that every one in England is well acquainted with the manners and customs of its natives, and since the enslaved negroes have, in general, been left in the same mental state they were found in, you must imagine the race here are a wild, inconsiderate, ignorant, strong passioned people. If there is any thing worse to be added to their character—if, as information gleams on them, they become subtle, malicious, pilfering (and as some would add ungrateful, though, God knows, *what* they have to be *grateful* for) all this must be placed to the account of *slavery*. I will go farther—if the Western districts of *Africa* at this day are not advanced in civilization, but, on the contrary, immersed in that " darkness visible" which is the worst of all conditions, where men adorn their savage institutions with the tinsel appendages of

civilization without possessing any of its solid
gold—this also is owing to *slavery*. The intellectual illumination which God hath lighted in
the nations of Europe, that it might " shine before men," has been placed " under a bushel,"
instead of giving " light unto all in the house,"
or family of mankind. But a better æra has
commenced. The Africans are recognized as
brethren, and Europe has commenced paying the
arrears of their heritage so long due to them.

You are aware that England has entered into
treaties with Spain, Portugal, and the Netherlands for the abolition of the slave trade. The
first named power (Spain) stipulated that from
the 22nd November 1817, her subjects should be
prohibited from carrying on the slave trade *north*
of the Equator, " upon any pretext or in any
manner whatever :" that the said trade should
be *entirely abolished* throughout her dominions on
the *30th of May*, 1820, and " that from and
" after that period it shall not be lawful for any
" of the subjects of the crown of Spain to pur-
" chase slaves, or to carry on the slave trade on
" *any part* of the coast of Africa, provided how-
" ever, that a term of five months, from the said
" date of the 30th of May, 1820, shall be
" allowed for completing the voyages of vessels

" which shall have cleared out lawfully previously
" to the said 30th May." As a compensation for
the losses consequent on the abolition of the
trade, the sum of £400,000 was paid by England
to Spain in February 1818, and his catholic
majesty issued a decree, in terms of the treaty,
prohibiting the slave trade throughout his
dominions.

The treaty with Portugal, dated July, 1817,
specifies *no period* for the *total* abolition of the
trade by that power, but it is stipulated that it
shall not be carried on *north* of the Equator ; and
the only traffic allowed to the *south* of the Equator is limited to the territories, possessed by the
crown of Portugal upon the coast of Africa.

The treaty with the king of the Netherlands
contains a stipulation on the part of that sovereign
to prohibit the slave trade from being prosecuted
by his subjects after the 25th January, 1819, and
he engages to enforce the prohibition " in the most
" effectual manner, and especially by penal laws
" the most formal, and, *in the event of the mea-*
" *sures already taken by the British government,*
" *and to be taken by that of the Netherlands, being*
" *found ineffectual or inefficient, the high contract-*
" *ing parties mutually engage to adopt such further*
" *measures, by legal provision or otherwise, as may*

" from time to time appear best calculated to pre-
" vent all their respective subjects from taking any
" share whatever in this nefarious traffic."

This latter stipulation shows the foresight and
energy of our government, in making provision
for tortuous attempts at illicit traffic, attempts
which, certainly, will be made and which, it is to
be feared, nothing but the universality of effort
by all civilized nations can prevent.   The British
government have erected barricades wherever
their influence extended, having first set an example of forbearance and disinterestedness which
the magnitude of their colonial concerns rendered
most forcible, both as an answer to the insinua-
tion of sinister motives (which foreigners are too
apt to ascribe to the exertions of England) but
also as an appeal, and incentive to the lingering
philanthropy of the world.   With Spain, Portugal, and the Netherlands, they have formed
treaties and provided for their execution by the
establishment of commissions at the *Havana, Rio
Janeiro, Surinam,* and *Sierra Leone,* consisting of
two commissary judges, and two commissioners
of arbitration, one of each being named by his
Britannic majesty and the others by the sove-
reigns of the respective territory.   These commissions are empowered to decide, without
appeal, on the legality of detentions of slave

ships by the cruisers of the different powers and
were established, by mutual concession, as checks
upon that bias, which the interest of the colonies
so strongly raises in their *local* governments, to
connive at the continuance of a traffic which every
one here tells you is absolutely essential to the
existence of this and every West India island.
Were you to see the half-cultivated, half-peopled
state of this important island, you would conceive
how strongly urged the point of abolition must
have been on a government by no means insensible to its value as a colony, and its merits on the
score of fidelity ; and, let me add, were you fully
acquainted with that punctilious pride which
characterizes the Spaniards, you would judge no
ordinary effort of *quid pro quo* negociation could
have induced them to admit a *foreign* tribunal to
exercise jurisdiction over and amongst them.
The more plastic Frenchman has refused to be
bound by treaty, or to allow of our taking a judi-
cial station on his territory, and the government
of the United states have done the same, solely
on the ground that it would be incompatible with
the feelings and spirit of an independent country.
The effect of this want of general compact is very
observable. It makes, what ought to be an im-
mutable law of nations, as it is of nature, merely
a local enactment subject to the versatility of

policy and opinion. Thus the *United States*, notwithstanding their high-sounding professions, have
within the present year, sanctioned the existence
and *necessity* of slavery in the new state of
Missouri. From whence do they conceive the
required supply of enslaved labourers is to come,
which may be necessary for the cultivation of an
immense tract as yet only faintly dotted with
population? Assuredly from that shore to which
they profess to extend a philanthropic immunity.
Thus also *French* slave traders are bringing cargoes to this island, though *France* professes to
carry on the traffic solely for the supply of her
own possessions. As long, therefore, as a single
nation withholds her acquiescence to a *total* abolition it is, I conceive, perfectly impossible for
England to prevent the slave trade from ravaging
Africa and outraging humanity. Though she
has taken the lead in the great cause, she
cannot *dictate*. By an over exertion of her power
and influence she would weaken their effects and
raise odium where she was planting charity. It
is from a judicious consideration of this consequence, and from a due regard to her political
relations, that a difference exists in the stipula-
tions of the treaties upon this subject. England
laid her basis broadly down—" the abolition of

the slave trade." To this proposition Spain, in
1814, (when flushed with the clearance of the
Peninsula from invaders and the return of her
monarch) answered—that she would take it
" into *consideration*, with the *deliberation* which
" the state of her possessions in America de-
" mands." But, as something was due to a
government which had exerted itself so stre-
nuously in her behalf, she engaged " to prohibit
" her subjects from carrying on the slave trade
" for the purpose of supplying any islands or
" possessions, excepting those appertaining to
" Spain ; and to prevent by effectual measures
" and regulations, the protection of the Spanish
" flag being given to foreigners who may en-
" gage in this traffic, whether subjects of his
" Britannic majesty, or of any other state or
" power."

This was something to gain, but it was not all
that England sought. It was the *apex* of the
wedge, which she continued impelling, till the
resisting mass was cloven. In 1817 the treaty
was signed and ratified by which Spain renounced
the slave trade, which was fostering her maritime
commerce, enriching her treasury, and augmenting the wealth and power of her firmest depend-
encies. The critical state of the majority of her

ultramarine dominions, her domestic difficulties, and the necessity of maintaining her European alliances aided this result.

The king of Portugal seated in his vast American territories, which nature has made one of her richest treasuries, where the rock and the cultivatable soil are alike productive, only required population to draw forth the wealth they are stored with. The Brazils had ceased to be an European dependence; its wants, therefore, were not of a secondary nature, and unhappily, the slave trade had become one. Possessed also of colonies on the African coast, it could not be expected that she would at once nullify her independence, and calmly give up, without equivalent, her power in Africa, and her expectations in America. And what equivalent could England give for the resignation of this last, for the breaking up of an empire; or what arguments, founded on social benevolence, could prevail against a system fraught, it is true, with moral evil, but producing political good? These, one would think, must be insuperable obstacles, but England has overcome them so far as to restrict the Portugueze slave trade at present, and to stipulate for its abolition at an early future.

The Netherlands stood differently related both to America and to England. To the last

she owes in pure gratuity, her colonial possessions, and her political affinity is closer than that
of any other power.   It is from this that the
treaty respecting the abolition, between these
two nations, bears the character rather of a
private arrangement than a public compact, and
provision for a series of preventive regulations
is made, which effectually unites the two powers
in continuous exertion.

I wish to my soul that I could carry on this
diplomatic summary, and name every nation in
this truly *holy alliance*.   But England is not idle,
and one day the social compact will be perfected,
and her statesmen receive the civic crowns of
Africa.   But till the period of this general
accordance, I repeat, it is vain to expect that
Africa will be civilized, or her people suffer less
from mercenary outrage.   If it were not that I
should grate the feelings of the ardent abolition-
ist, I would add, they will suffer *more*.

The international regulations for the seizing
and adjudging illicit slave traders will be serviceable no doubt, but the amount of that service de-
pends upon, as it were, the *fortune of war*; they
may or may not be captured.   In the event of the
second supposition, the local laws meet them, and
presuming them to be executed with a fidelity
not to be swayed by private interests, or an

opinion of their being adverse to those of the
community, yet we well know, that, restrict as we
will and as we *can*, there is no legislative enactment, however strongly guarded, but what is frequently evaded and dared. Within these few
months two Portugueze brigs with 566 slaves on
board entered, one, the small unfrequented port
of *Batabanò*, on the southern coast of this island,
the other the *Havana*, in violation of our treaty
with her nation. At the same moment, perhaps,
a Spanish trader might be visiting the Brazil
coast in a similar way. They are punishable *in*
their respective dominions, *under the treaties* between England and Portugal, and England and
Spain, *if captured*, but they are not punishable
by the national code of the countries they visited.
Three French vessels have also, within the period
above-mentioned, entered the port of Havana with
slaves ;—but they are not tangible either way.
So much for *evasion ;* and as to *daring*, no country
in the world has coasts so well calculated for
smuggling as the island of Cuba, nor do I believe
there is any other traffic in the world that holds
out such strong inducements to illicit endeavours
as that in slaves. A short statement will show
you the ground of my opinion. In the year previous to the date of the treaty, viz. in 1816,
17,733 negroes were imported into the Havana

from Africa. The value of goods, dollars, and
stores carried thither, and which returned in exchange the *net* number of 17,733 slaves (for the
mortality of the Spanish *middle* passage is usually
very great) amounted to 643,852 dollars. The
custom house valuation was, 150 dollars per head,
or 2,659,950 dollars total, which, with the deduction of duties and incidental expences, would
leave about 100 per cent. profit, but as the custom
house valuation was under the real, the profit
would approach nearer to 150 per cent. After
the ratification of the treaty for the abolition, not
only were the importing duties nearly entirely
taken off, but the value of slaves in the island rose
prodigiously, at the present time averaging 500
dollars per head, and prime slaves 600 dollars.
On the other hand as the value of slaves rose,
the articles usually required in trafficking for them
on the African coast, fell, as the anticipation of
the demand soon ceasing, caused the holders to
throw them plentifully on the market. Thus negroes were *purchased*, probably, *a third cheaper*,
in Africa, and sold *three times higher* in the
Havana; so that if the same value of goods that
was shipped from hence in 1816 (viz. 643,852
dollars) was carried to Africa, by vessels sailing
from this port previous to the 30th May, 1820,
the return of slaves ought to be, in numbers

23,644 and in value above 11,000,000 dollars!!
Let it be recollected also, that after the legitimate
traffic is terminated, the value of slaves will be
annually rising, till it attains the maximum,
which the planters' profit or love of speculation
may allow it to reach, and, consequently, that
the temptation to the illicit trader will be
strengthening in proportion. In an island of such
extent as this, with nearly 2,000 miles of coast,
presenting inlets on all sides to adventurous navi-
gation, and a tract of country lying thin and se-
vered as to population, so that the hand of government can scarcely grasp it, we must expect that
smuggling in slaves will be carried on to a great
extent. *Smuggling in slaves!* The very name
gives rise to ideas of terrific cruelty and remorse-
less cupidity!

Well, but you exclaim, how are we to prevent
this? *We*, my friend! *We* cannot do every thing
in the world that requires spirited exertion, dis-
interested feeling and enlightened notions. *We*
were the *last* to begin a slave trade and the *first*
to abolish it.* *We*, the possessors of the major
part of the colonies—with a greater interest at
stake than any other, than *all other*, nations—*we*

* From our great sacrifices as well as exertions *Denmark* will
yield us this station.

have set the example, completely abolished the traffic, watch with all the jealousy of honour against every infringement *amongst ourselves*—have besought—have *bought*, the concurrence of other powers in the work of humanity, and continue supporting agents in various parts to watch over and protect its progress. What more can we do, consistent with the *independent* character of other nations or the unassuming propriety of our own ?　The slave trade has been nearly 300 years in action, has been *nationalized* and *budgetted* in Africa itself, and it is vain to expect that we should overthrow at once what has been so long systematized in two quarters of the globe.

As far as I am able to judge, I think that the means hitherto taken, may, in a great degree, diminish the number of negroes brought from Africa, but will not *abolish* the trade, and most probably, will cause a deeper infliction of misery on those unfortunate beings the objects of illicit traffic. If at any period a breach should take place in the pacific relations of Great Britain, with any of the powers, to whom she now delegates commissioners for abolishing the slave trade, the consequence will be the dissolution of the commission and the renewal of the traffic. Such an event is, happily, not likely to occur, but the *possibility* of it gives a temporary character to the

mode of abolition and involves the point too much
with the vacillations of policy. Till *the principle
of abolition* is written in the code of nations as it
is in that of nature, we must expect humanity to
be outraged. Stamp the slave-trader with the
name of *pirate*, pursue him with deadly rigour—
make him judicable in *any* part of the civilized
world;—endeavour, at the same time, through
the medium of *educated natives*, by colonizing the
dangerous and burthensome West India black
corps and by legitimate commerce, to gradually
humanize the coasts of Africa, and then, in the
course of years, we may wear down the slave trade
and raise up the force of opinion against it on the
very spot where its markets now stand.

It is only of late years that the Spaniards have
been *carriers* in the slave trade. Eleven years
after the discovery of America, viz. in 1503, they
commenced purchasing negroes from the Portugueze; but, in 1542, the traffic was *abolished* by
Charles 5th (1st of Spain) *notwithstanding* which,
in 1569, there were *twenty-two thousand negroes*
in the island of Santo Domingo only. To this increase, England, (who commenced the trade in
1563) was a principal contributor, and, finally,
by the *assiento* contract, after the peace of Utrecht,
she became the *sole carrier* for a time, till in 1789
the traffic was thrown open.

During the first ten subsequent years (viz. from 1789 to 1799) 41,500 negroes were imported into this island, or rather more than 4000 annually. During the next four years, 34,500 were imported, or about 8,600 annually. From that time to the year of the abolition treaty (1817), being a period of 13 years, above 150,000 negroes were introduced, or more than 10,000 annually. In the years 1817, 1818, and 1819, there was a great increase of importation nearly 60,000 having been brought to the island during that period.

Thus in the last thirty years more than 200,000 negroes have been brought from Africa to this island, and it is no vague supposition to presume, that 50,000 more have perished in the transit.*— No comment is necessary.

I have told you that there are 370,000 people of colour in the island. Of these the *free* mulattoes and blacks rank first, more particularly in their own estimation. These beings (singular as it may seem to those ignorant of human nature)

---

* Many lamentable instances in proof of this calculation might be adduced. The Spanish law allows *five* slaves for every *two* tons, and though the number is fully completed on the coast of Africa, the average of import is *two* slaves *per ton!* One vessel loaded, sailed, lost nearly the whole of her cargo, returned to the coast and contrived from her spare stores to load a second time. She arrived at the *Hacana* with a proportion of only *one and a half slaves per ton!*

look down on those they are sprung from, if it be possible, with more contempt than the whites do, while they regard the latter with an envy, almost too natural to be condemned. Though tinted with the die of slavery, they possess certain privileges, here called *freedom*, but which have little analogy to the Europeon meaning of the word; they are unchained but the collar remains on their necks. They are subject to most of the restrictions imposed on the slave, such as respect carrying weapons, being out after dark without a lanthorn, &c. and they are equally deprived of information, their freedom by no means extending to their minds. Their condition is usually good, notwithstanding their extreme indolence. The high price of labour enables them to gain sufficient, by slight and discontinuous exertion, to pass nearly a third of their time in sleep or gambling. A free man of colour, who is a tolerable artificer, will make from *twelve reales* (6s. 9d.) to *three dollars* (13s. 6d.) per day, and this he earns rather by a sort of hysterical effort, than by *labour*. He will work half this day, a third of next, abandon his work the day after, and return as he feels the necessity. Perhaps in the middle of the work to be completed, he will leave his employer for another situated nearer his gaming haunts; no dependence is to be placed on him.

Those of this class who are domestics usually receive *six reales* (*3s.* 4½*d.*) per day. If free from the vice of gaming they are generally honest, but a restlessness under any sort of restraint seems to characterize them. They consider themselves hired for some specific piece of service, as a *cook*, as a *calesero* (or coachman), as a *porter*, &c.; beyond the precise line of their duty, it is difficult to obtain their assistance, and they put their commentary on the contract of hiring. Two or three days after you have engaged them, they will tell you that you require too many dishes on your table—want your *volante* (the carriage of the country) too often—or that you send too many messages. They quit you on the eve of a party, a drive out, or sealing a letter. Notwithstanding this, their service is preferable to that afforded by the gloomy slave, who knows he shall get nothing but harsh words and buffets for what he does, and who has no interest in exertion or prospect of its ending.

There are many coloured people whose freedom is the purchase of the extra earnings allowed them by law. These are the most valuable of their class and commonly continue in their course of industry as hawkers of market goods, and petty dealers in tobacco, &c. Those who reside in the country differ in little from the lower

order of whites with whom they maintain a perfect fellowship. Both descriptions are frequently
seen working together at the same trade, and I
regret to say, still more frequently, gambling
together. This vice and an immoderate love
of dress are the bane of the labouring class.
You would smile to see groups of black females
with silk stockings, satten shoes, muslin gowns,
French shawls, gold ear-rings and flowers in their
woollen head-dress, gallanted by black beaux,
with white beaver hats, English coats and gold-
headed canes, all smoking in concert like their
superiors. These are your washerwomen and
cobblers, festivalizing on a " *dias de dos cruces,*"
or a church holiday. The next day you will
have them at your door with some article of this
finery, which they are seeking a sale for, to pay
for the day's subsistence !

The distinction arising from holdiday array
is all this class of people can aspire to, or in
which they can vie with the whites. The principle of depression, universally acted on with
respect to them, keeps them down as a body, and
puts them aside from the race of honourable
emulation, excluding them from a course which
the indolent whites are seen merely walking over.
It is not to be wondered at, that the plant, which
is prevented from rising, should grow crooked.

The number of free people of colour in this island is nearly equal to the total amount of that class in *all* the islands together. This is attributable to the mildness of the Spanish slave code which softens the rigour of their hard destiny, in a way very different from what would have been expected from a nation, whose colonial enterprises have caused such waste of life and extent of misery amongst the Indian hordes. The facilities afforded the slave will, however, come more correctly in detail, under the summary which I shall now give you of his condition.

The slaves of Cuba must be considered either as *field labourers* or *domestics*, because in this more than any other island, the condition of these respective classes varies. Those employed in household duties will, of course, be expected to possess advantages, and to have been selected for qualities, not enjoyed by the others, and frequently, either from the good nature or negligence of their masters, live in a state of ease and comparative happiness. Pride and luxury have accumulated numbers round themselves; some, in the Havana, having no less than *sixty* household slaves, encumbering the ease they are meant to supply, and forming a grandeur which is more confusing than dazzling. There are, indeed, some wealthy proprietors, whom I gladly except, that are surrounded by these hordes, less for state than from a wish not to alienate those born under their roof, and bearing their name.*

These domestics, born in hereditary service, are commonly the associates of their young masters during their juvenile years and, not uncommonly, the pets of their mistresses. They are seen sprawling and sporting at the feet of their owners with the young whites of the family, and are accustomed to the free range of the house with their associate lordlings, thus acquiring habits of familiarity not easily got rid of when the nature of their service is changed. This occurs when their white fellows become masters and require their companions to be menials. They are, then, either suffered to serve with a kind of familiar air, which to a casual observer looks very like insolence, or otherwise, are repulsed and commanded harshly, a treatment which they feel keenly, and are sure to testify. But, in whatever way they are treated by their masters, the love of liberty soon renders them restless. They see numbers of their colour enjoy freedom, and the laws sanction their attempt at attaining the same immunity.

Every slave, under the Spanish colonial law, who tenders his master the sum he was bought

---

* The slaves are baptised by the name of their first owner.

at, is entitled to enfranchisement, *nor can his
master refuse it.* It is equally permitted him to
purchase *a portion of his freedom,* by instalments,
as his ability allows, being then said to be
coartado or *cut,* and such are, in consequence, entitled to a license to work where and with whom
they please, paying to their master a *real* per
day for every hundred dollars remaining of their
value beyond the instalment they have paid.
Many who are not *coartado* are allowed by their
owners to labour where they please under similar conditions, by which means an industrious
slave may in a few years procure sufficient to
ransom himself. The excellence of such a regulation it is easy to appreciate. The permission
to purchase freedom by portions is both a wise
and merciful policy. It satisfies the master with
a high interest, during the period the slave is
working out his freedom, and it imbues the
latter with habits of cheerful industry while he
is, as it were, knocking off his chain link by link.
Another regulation, in the spirit of the former, is
the allowance to a slave, who is discontented with
the treatment of his owner, to demand a *carta* or
license to be sold, or, in other words, to change
his service. In this case, however, the owner
may place what value he pleases on his slave.

It sounds very singularly to a stranger in the

West Indies to be addressed with the words—
" *Pray, Sir, will you buy me ?*"   For my part I
felt an awkward sensation when first addressed
thus by a *fellow-creature*, but the frequency of
these questions has now become agreeable to me,
because I view it as arising from my being an
Englishman, a native of that country whose
exertions in the cause of the African race will, I
trust, be venerated by the *civilized descendants* of
those, whom they are directed to save from the
double bondage of slavery and barbarism.

Added to the ameliorating regulations of
slavery, which I have just mentioned, are those
which *enforce* the natural obligation of the owner
of a slave to support him and clothe him decently.
Further than these, what can *laws* do ?   They
cannot convert tyranny into wildness, or tear off
the fibres of prejudice, which are woven round
the heart of a slave owner.   They recognize as
a principle, that men, equal in the sight of God,
are unequal in the sight of each other, and have
stamped this inequality by a deeper brand than
nature can sanction, or humanity should allow,
raising a despotism where nature only intended
a federal dependance, and investing civilization
with rights which its principles cannot accord
with.   In the societies of Europe, though the
degree or rank is fixed, every individual has it in
his power by merit or good fortune to change the

one he was born in ; but here, in the insular countries of America, the majority of the population are stamped with *lasting* degradation, forcibly kept down from elevating themselves, and thus acquire a stoop of character which their white lords firmly believe is the genuine impress of nature. Thus, common minds, finding themselves *born masters* of beings who were *born slaves*, think, (I use the word in its popular sense) that nature made them both so, and sway their sceptres with cool despotism *de jure divino*. " Oh ! nature ! Oh ! thou goddess !" how would these, worse than Pagans, personify thee ? As a stout, though meagre, sallow-faced, sunk-eyed, huge whiskered *African trader !*

The laws I have detailed apply to both classes of slaves, though circumstances make their benefits less available to the *field* than the *domestic* negroes. In one respect they are all equal—in the state of utter ignorance they are kept in. No where is the axiom better understood, that, *knowledge is power*.

The *field* negroes are either *bozales*, or slaves sent thither, and retained there, who are either too dull to be used as artificers and domestics, or whose faults in these latter capacities are punished by this species of banishment. To be sent " *al monte*" is the severest punishment a domestic negro can be threatened with. This is suffi-

cient to show the distinction between their conditions.

The parts of the island where the *ingenio's*, or
sugar plantations, and the *caffetales,* or coffee
estates, lie, are remote from the Havana and
towns where the proprietors reside.   They are
consequently left to the management of *overseers,*
men, in all the islands, usually of indifferent cha-
racters and desperate fortunes, or if they are not,
are, at least, in that rank of life where prejudice
is less likely to be checked by education, or feeling, to have attained any degree of refinement.
The slaves committed to their charge depend
entirely on temper, and are too remote from the
society of their more favored fellows to learn the
rights the laws have given them.   From their locality they are also debarred from the advantages
of extra labour, or a charge of service ; they are
penned up amidst the mountains, and the only
remedy for suffering is, either patience or revolt.
Not a year passes without instances of the latter.
Last winter a body of 700 took to the hills, and it
was two months before the military sent against
them could compel them to surrender.   It is vain
to talk of men being well treated when they risk
their lives to ameliorate their condition.

In the *Havana,* besides other sources of fortune, there is a lottery, drawn monthly, where
for five reales (or 2s. 9¼d.) a share may be

obtained. This procures freedom for many, but is still more serviceable as a recruiting depot for the plantations. *Five reales* are first to be obtained by the candidate for fortune. He at last obtains them, tries his fortune, and fails of success. Theft and gaming are next ventured on, and drunkenness, of course, follows. The unfortunates incur chastisement, become sullen and indifferent and draw down upon themselves a harshness which augments the evils of their condition. They fly from their masters, are retaken and sent to labour on the plantations where they disseminate discontent, and wait for the opportunity of revolt.

Such is a summary of the state of the slaves in this island. If happiness is to be considered as a constituent of prosperity, it is impossible to assert a land of slavery to be prosperous. The two colours are in perpetual dread of each other. The indolence of the whites is met by the indifference of the blacks; luxury is sickened and repose agitated, while delicacy and feeling fly from scenes where they are every moment liable to be disturbed. Thus live the motley population of a West India island, holding nothing in common but a faith, whose peculiar doctrine is that they will all ultimately meet together—*in concord and in Heaven.*

LETTER III.

Re-establishment of the Constitution—detail of its consequences.
Situation; territorial division and government of the island.
Administration of Justice; number of Counsel, or *Abogado's*.
Junta Provincial. Delegation to the Cortes. The City of
Havana—described. Yellow Fever; some of the causes of
its prevalence. Rents of houses; construction of them.
Shops. Public buildings. Churches and Convents. Ecclesiastical population. University of *San Geronimo*. Schools
and establishments for public instruction. Education and
mental character of a Spaniard. Clergy; their constitutional
bias. Archbishoprick of Cuba; churches in its diocese.
Bishoprick of Havana; churches in its diocese. Revenues
of the Bishop and Clergy. Division of the City. Garrison
and militia. *Compania's Urbana's*—their number and use.
Frequency of assassination.

———————

I HAVE introduced you to my friends here; it
is high time we should proceed to visit them in
their dwellings, and learn how they live. On
our way, it would be adviseable to give you some
idea of the politics of the island, for the effervescence of feeling is so great at present, that we
shall hear nothing in private but discussions on
public affairs and probably find the mass of the

Havanero's collected in the *Plaza*, or great square, attending some constitutional ceremony.

Every thing now is *constitutional*. The burst of liberty, which, after six years of arbitrary government, broke the political slumber of Spain and its provinces, rolled as loud and as sudden on the ears of the *Cubano's* as the thunder which is now pealing above me. No community was ever kept more completely out of hearing of all that could interest them, than this. Public news came thoroughly sifted of every particle of anti-despotism, through the government press ; and, though a free trade necessarily brought information, it rested, like the *miasmata* of fever, chiefly on the sea-shore. It seemed as if the body-politic was like the body-natural, that the *head* was the sole seat of intellect, for the state of the country, was secreted in the public departments, not even a map of the island being allowed to be published.* It soon, however, appeared that " the very body *thought*."

---

* The government of the Havana was not ill-provided with the apparatus of despotic power, as the following :—

" Extract of the report made by the deputation of the Junta Provincial respecting the prisons of the Havana, May 22nd, 1820," will show. " In the *Cabana* they were horror-struck at finding dark dungeons, damp and unhealthy, which have been hitherto employed in afflicting humanity. They found prisoners

On the 15th April 1820, a merchant vessel from *Corunna* brought a copy of the Madrid Gazette of the 7th of March, containing an account of the accession of the king of Spain to the constitution of 1812. This news transpiring, the governor found it advisable to publish a *Diario Extraordinario*, in which, after acknowledging the receipt of such intelligence, he added "*But his excellency the captain general knows no other guide than the will of his sovereign and he waits it's expression.*" The people, and more particularly the military, immediately took the alarm, interpreting this notice as an expression of disinclination to the constitutional regime, and crowding together into the *Plaza de Armas* where the government-house is situated, they loudly demanded the captain-general to take an immediate

who had been detained there for many years in rigorous confinement without condemnation, solely on account of official intimation of their being suspected of want of fealty to the government of *New Spain*. In the castle of the *Moro*, in the *Punta*, in *El Principe*, the Dragoon barracks, and those of the White Militia, *San Telmo*, and the Artillery; the places destined for criminals are well ventilated, dry and spacious; but the prisons of the *Arsenal* are narrow galleries; and those of *La Fuerza**
and the Black barracks are dark and want air."

* La Fuerza or the citadel is the governor's palace. General Renovoles died in the dungeons of La Cabana the same day the report was dated.

D

oath of adherence to the new order of things. This strong indication of public spirit compelled the governor to accede to their wishes, and accordingly on the evening of the 16th. (on the morning of which day his notification, as above, was published,) he took the oath required, and was followed by the other public authorities.

It was curious to see how suddenly this city of statutes started into life. The very slaves, as if refreshed by the air of freedom that blew round them, seemed elated with the change. The first thought was to establish the *lapida,* or pillar of the constitution, which, being a piece of *political superstition,* happily united the two uppermost ideas of the people. The next fundamental proceeding was to alter all the royal emblems and names into others of a more popular kind. The *Plaza de Fernando Septimo* became the *Plaz de la Constitucion ;* the *Real Lateria* became *La Lateria Constitucional,* and the *Real Hacienda,* or *Royal Domains* were titled *Hacienda Publica.* Then followed the *desofficing* the *royal* Alcalde's, Regidores (who, in the Havana, had paid *eight thousand dollars* for their situations) and other municipal officers, re-instating those who held those places under the rule of the *Cortes.*

The press, now possessed of freedom, commenced pouring forth odes, sonnets, advices, essays, and every species of composition by every species of author. No less than fourteen periodical papers made their appearance in a few weeks, besides a prodigious number of sheets and half sheets, all filled with politics and details of the abuses that existed under the late form of government.* Unhappily most of these works are tinctured with personality, which has given rise to much threatening and counter-threatening and afforded constant employment to the *Junta de Censura*, (or board for censuring defamatory publications) in seizing objectionable works.

The strong spirit excited against the arbitrary exercise of power, has, unfortunately, raised an opposition even to its constitutional employ. Doubts have been continually rising about the extent of particular authority, and, as the appeal is always made to the people in pretty strong terms, the officers of government are diffident of using it. A kind of *Saturnalia* exists at present ; the people have received liberties and *take* more.

* The titles of some of these may afford an idea of their style and contents. *El Mosquito* (The Mosquito).—*La Avrspa* (The Wasp).—*La Mosca* (The Fly).—*El Esquife* (The Skiff) —*El Sartre Contitucional* (The Constitutional Tailor).—*Los rugidos de un leon Africano* (Roarings of an African Lion).—*Rasgas brillantes de arbitriedad* (Brilliant Deeds of Despotism), besides an infinity of *Proclamo's, Manifiesto's,* &c. by private individuals " *á mis conciudanas, ilustres Habanero's.*"

The opinion of the government, as to the tendency of this spirit may be inferred, from the frequent repetition of its assurance that "nothing is farther from the thoughts of the heroic people of this island, than division from the interest of the Peninsula, notwithstanding the efforts made by a few ignorant individuals to persuade them that they lie separate." On the contrary, I am inclined to think that the " *heroic people*"* are the only persons who entertain such notions, and that the *sense* of the island is counter to that "vaulting ambition" which would certainly " overleap itself." The independence of Cuba will meet with many obstacles, if it ever takes place. At present the amount and mixed nature of its population will prevent it standing singly. The very attempt would prove its incapacity. As to the future, whatever population it may possess, it stands so equivocally between the territories of two powers whose rivalry is yearly strengthening, that its jeopardy seems to be great. The maternal tie will be loosened by time, and the examples of colonial independence, which this quarter of the globe powerfully affords ; but as a *single* state, I must doubt if there be a basis wide

---

* There is much *Napoleonism* in public addresses, " *Illustrious—noble—heroic*" are the usual appellatives employed in the most trifling *parish* business.

enough for its erection and the least political gust
would have a fearful effect upon its tenuity.

These are speculations I had determined not
to make. My purpose was to give you a summary account of this island, and its inhabitants,
without venturing on political prophesy, which
the mutable age we live in is peculiarly unfavor-
able to. I will resume it by describing the island
under its new form of government.

The figure of the island of Cuba is a bent ob-
long, arching towards the Florida stream, from
the north western coast of Santo Domingo, and
spreading across the mouth of the gulf of Mexico
to the point of *cape Catoche*. From east to west
a mountainous ridge runs nearly the whole length
of the island, from which spring a great number
of rivers, but whose course, north and south, to
the sea is too short to admit of their arriving at
magnitude. One or two (such as the Rio's Sa-
gua la grande, Giguia Jaruco, and Santa Crioz)
allow small vessels to work up to load about
a league from the sea.

The island (which lies between 73° 50′ and
85° 30′ west longitude, and 23° 20′ and 19° 40′
north latitude) is as you may compute, nearly
700 miles long, but little more than 50 or 60
broad. It is popularly divided into two parts
by a supposed line drawn, north and south, along

the eastern border of the province of Havana ;
the tract to the west being termed " *Vuelta
abaxo*" that to the east " *Vuelta arriba.*" The
legitimate division is into three provinces,
Havana, Cuba, and *Puerto Principe,* over each
of which there is a governor ; but that of the
Havana, being also captain-general of the
island, gives that province precedence. Each
province is divided into *Partido's* or *portions,*
(usually from one to two leagues square) of
which the province of *Havana* contains 76, that
of *Cuba* 32, and *Puerto Principe* 12. These
include only the inhabited part of the island, a
vast tract in the interior and the southern coast
lying as yet unnamed and unappropriated.

Over each *partido* there is a *Capitan de Partido,*
immediately subject to the governor of the province. His duty is to preserve the public peace,
keep the roads free from obstruction, and publish
and enforce the proclamations of government.
Those towns, however, in the *partido* which
possess *ayuntamiento's,* or corporate bodies, are
exempt from his jurisdiction. These govern
their own district, subject to the *junta provincial*
or assembly of the province, to whom they are
obliged to furnish an annual statement of the
collection and disbursement of what public
money they are entrusted with. Of these *ayun-*

tamiento's (the members of which are elected by the inhabitants of the town) there are 42 in the province of Havana, every place which possesses a thousand souls being entitled to this municipal right.

The *partido's* and privileged towns are further divided into *parroguia's*, or parishes, every parish having a *cura* or rector, and, in the election of deputies to the *cortes* and the *junta provincial*, choosing a delegate to assist at the electoral meeting of the *Partido*.*

The administration of justice in the *Partido's* rests with the *Alcalde's* resident in the different towns. Their authority extends, however, merely to hearing and determining (with the assistance of *two* good and honest men, together with an *escribano* or attorney) all civil demands not exceeding *one hundred dollars*, and all criminal matters, touching peace and morals, which only merit light correction. Matters of higher consequence are cognizable by the *audiencia* or high court of justice, consisting of a *regente*, nine *ministro's*, and two *fiscals*, who have authority

* For electoral purposes the province of Havana is divided into 12 Partido's,—Havana, Santiago de Compostela; Bejucal; S. Antonio Abad; Guanajay; Guanabacoa; Pinal del Rio; Guines; Jamco; Matanzas; Santa Clara; Trinidad. These comprise the lesser partido's.

over the territorial judges, receive appeals in
matters of tithes and regulate the admission of
abogado's, or counsel, and of *escribano's,* both of
whom only practice upon paper ; the administration of justice (notwithstanding the constitutional reform) being conducted in the *closet,* and
all evidence, in cases both civil and criminal, as
well as arguments and pleadings in the same,
being arranged and composed by the *abagodo's*
and *escribano's* in their offices.

While I am on the subject, I cannot help
interrupting my statistics by observing on the
love of litigation shown by the *Havanero's.*
Dublin itself can scarcely vie with it in the
number of *abogado's* or counsel. The island
can boast of above *one hundred and fifty* of these
"learned gentlemen," besides a flock of *escribano's,*
and who, to do them justice, are as industrious a
race as any in the old world. Their course of
practise, as I have observed, is of a *quieter* tenor
than ours; they cannot figure out of their
" *estudio*'s" which they, now and then, remind
the public are situated at *numero* so-and-so, *Calle
de*———— at the right hand corner, next to the
Tienda de ropa, and facing the convent of some of
the orders ! Justice here partakes rather of the
laxity of the climate; she does not move from
her seat, and is very slow in her proceedings. A

circuit with the thermometer at 80°, would, indeed, be tremendous, and when the feverish irritability and play of passions are considered, which usually invade the bands of itinerant *brief-hunters*, a wholesome mortality might be expected on a *West India circuit.*

Perhaps, now the people are become politicians, the *excitement* of litigation will not be in such demand. Hitherto the *elections* have been serviceable in this way. You are aware that the colonies of Spain are admitted to a share in the representation as *integral* parts of the nation.* Locally they have only a *Diputacion*, or Junta Provincial, consisting of *nine* members, of whom the *governor* and *intendant* of the province make a part, the other *seven* being elected by the inhabitants. At the end of two years, *four* of the seven make way for the same number of new members; in two years more the remaining *three* are displaced also. This board is similar to the *council* of our colonies.

This summary will give you knowledge enough to allow of your entering into society at the Havana. We will proceed thither without more delay, therefore.

The city of *La Havana* lies, as almost every

* The island sends three deputies to the Còrtes.

West India town does, on the flat coast of a bay.
On approaching the city by sea, you behold a
narrow inlet, on the left of which a high rocky
prominence is surmounted by a fortress called,
El Morro. This is a regular and exceeding
strong work, whose majestic spread and elevation
of masonry, studded with cannon, flags and military figures, in the full blaze of sunshine, presents
a noble and truly imposing sight. On the right
point of the inlet stands a small square fort called
La Punta, very inferior in strength and appearance to the *Morro.* On sailing between them
you are hailed by a sentry and required to give
your name and port of departure, so *conversable*
is the width of the inlet, which, having shot
through, you glide into a harbour, or rather bay,
extending deep and broad nearly a mile across,
and three inland. On the right shore behind *La
Punta,* stands the *Havana,* presenting its thickly
built edifices of stone, interspersed with numerous
spires of churches and convents, behind the walls
which surround it. There is an air of solid age
which the town presents from the harbour, that
gives it a *grand* appearance ; the maritime bustle
gives it *interest* ; the idea of wealth and luxury
is strongly impressed on you, and, as you listen
to the rattling of carriages and the strains of gaie-
ty, and gaze at the peculiar brightness and glitter

which distinguish tropical scenes, you forget that
the city before you is the banquetting place of
death. The situation of the *Havana* is but too
favourable to the propagation and retention of
disease, being, in addition to its fortifications,
enclosed on all sides with a circle of rising ground
which precludes the free circulation of air and
causes a stagnant cloud of fetid vapour, exhaled
from a crowded population and the marshy shores
of the harbour, to hang continually over it. The
direful yellow fever (here called "*Elvomito negro*"
from the final symptom) is found to be nearly entirely confined in its ravages to the sea shore;
at any rate there is not such conflux of human
beings in the inland towns, and there is consequently, both a diminished cause of pestilence and
food for its maintenance. The foreign vessels
which arrive here suffer greatly. Whole crews
are swept off within a few weeks of their arrival,
and great difficulty is found in procuring hands
for the home passage. Indeed there is scarcely
an European who escapes an attack, and multitudes of young ardent adventurers are hurried
off from their earthly hopes with a rapidity that
would appal you; but, here, as in the ranks of
battle, the survivors, habituated to the dropping
around them, scarcely think of turning to note the
victim.

On passing the *sea-gate* you become sensible of one great cause of disease, from the insufferable stench of the stores of dried beef and fish which are imported for the sustenance of the blacks. A multitude of narrow streets open to your eye, each contributing to the congress of smells, by their want of sewers and paving, the holes, worn in the ground by wheels and horses, being carefully filled up with offal. Add to this the swarm of *black population*, and you have a very fair *olfactory* catalogue.

The narrow streets are formed of large solid houses, usually one story high, the ground floors of which are commonly occupied as shops and warehouses. If it be a merchants, the counting houses are up stairs, and the *patio*, or court yard, in the centre of the building (round which all the rooms are ranged, opening into balconies) is filled with produce and effects. In the passage from the outward gate to the *patio*, sits a *yellow white man* to *eye* and answer strangers. You would think him made by *Maillardet*, so stationary you find him, so perpetually with his *çigar* in his mouth and so mechanically regular in the three measured puffs and the gradual elevation of his eyelids, which invariably take place before he answers you.

A house of this description, you will be astonished to hear, lets from 8000 to 14,000 dollars per annum, or in pounds English, from £1800 to £3150 !! But you will recollect that the *Havana* is a regular fortification, and that *no more houses than those already in it can be built within its walls ;* that the influx of commerce has been sudden and its profits enormous; and that both fashion and trade have localities. Beyond the walls, houses are not so exorbitant, though even there, as that situation is considered as possessing some immunity from the fever, they are very high in rent.

The dwellings of the nobility and gentry are similar in construction to those I have described. To the street they present a plain stone front with a broad passage opening at the side, in which the *volante*, or carriage, stands. If there are apartments on the ground floor, the windows are large and high, barred with iron, without any glazing, and usually have curtains hung within, to prevent curiosity and dust from being too intrusive. Above are similar windows opening into a balcony that runs the breadth of the house. The roof is tiled, and of course, in this tropical region, has no plume of chimnies crowning its top.

Most commonly, even in the houses of the nobility, the ground floor is let out for shops, or at least nooks are opened at the corners of the house for that purpose. This relieves the heaviness which would otherwise characterize the streets. There are many houses and shops that have only a ground floor, which of course have more airyness in their appearance, especially as the latter universally have boards over their doors with signs painted on them, as little indicative, however of what they contain as the pole of a barber is of his suds and razor. Thus one may see the figure of a hero, blazoned forth duly with *mustachia's, whiskers,* a huge cocked hat and a Goliah sword, underneath which, to prevent mistake, is inscribed—" *El Hèroe Espanol.*" On entering the place it designs, you behold a meagre wizen-faced tailor florishing his shears on a shopboard. Next door is a jeweller, or rather silversmith, whose portal is decorated with an interesting portrait of a *caballero,* with one hand on his heart, extending the other towards another equally well-drest *caballero.* This is the sign of " *El buen amigo*"—the *good friend,* and on seeing it, you might be disposed to enter cordially and purchase without fear of imposition, but, alas, one probably finds that here, as in other parts of the world, the *outward profession* is very different from the *internal disposition !*

The public buildings, such as the Captain General's residence, the *Intendencia,* the cathe-

dral, churches, convents, &c. show little architectural skill. The first is a fine building, in the
midst of a large open space called *Plaza de armas*,
having a long portico in front, under which the
merchants assemble as in an Exchange. In other
respects the plan is the same as in the other great
houses, except that the lower floor, instead of
being converted into warehouses, serves for the
city *prison*, thus affording a practical exposition
of government and a novel piece of architectural
morality.

The churches, and convents are solidly built,
but have rather an humble exterior. The deco-
ration of the one and the tenants of the other are
not exactly in the same style. The altars are
richly piled with gold and silver adorned with
well-executed images, large as life, splendidly
arrayed in costly garments, "*which moth and rust
doth corrupt and* (as has frequently happened)
which thieves break through to steal." Amongst
these, elevated into *divinity*, stands conspicu-
ously eminent, the virgin wife of the poor car-
penter of Nazareth, the blessed but the humble
instrument of God's mercy to mankind. Covered
with those treasures, which, though here used as
celestial ornaments, the Apostle tells us find *no
entrance into heaven*, she is exalted at the high
altar with crowds of devotees prostrate before

her, turning their backs on a drooping image in a corner extended on a cross and crowned only with thorns! Except for the presence of this neglected figure, you might conceive yourself in the temple at *Ephesus* before the shrine of *Diana*.

The convents are only 12 in number but are not well stocked. The ecclesiastical population of the Havana is 417. The whole island contains 1034 of this class, male and female, so that the church militant here is not particularly well officered. The monastic orders are *useful*, in some degree, by having established schools in their several convents for the rudiments of knowledge. In the convent of *preaching friars* (established in 1723) there is a kind of *university*, called of St. Jerome, with a long list of chancellor, rectors, counsellors, commissaries, fiscal, treasurer, *master of the ceremonies*, and professors of *theology, sacred canons, civil jurisprudence, medicine, philosophy, mathematics* and *humanity*. In February last the professor of mathematics notified by public advertisement that he had not been able to proceed in his course because *no scholar had appeared at the time of opening!* Beside this there is a royal foundation for 24 scholars called the "*royal seminary of San Carlos* and *San Ambrosio.*" The *economical society* of the Havana, at the head of which is the intelligent and amiable *D. Alexandro*

Ramirez, *superintendente general* of the island, has exerted itself arduously in promoting and diffusing knowledge. Schools on the royal British system have been opened, and also others for gratuitous tuition in political economy, painting and drawing, and the training of ten deaf and dumb pupils. Lectures on anatomy and chemistry have been established likewise, and prizes are annually distributed to those students who excel. All this has been effected in the last three years, and under the direction of the above named gentleman. I regret to read in the account of the progress of these institutions, written by the secretary of the economical society, that, some " se hallen menos concurridas que *al principio*, en que, *por razon de la novedad* hubo grande afluencia de jovenes"—"there was a less numerous attendance than at *first*, when a great many youths were attracted by the *novelty* of the thing." The manager of the Theatre has frequently occasion to make the same remark on the representations of his " *comedia's famosas*."

I believe the Spaniards to be advancing very rapidly towards intellectual day. After a long night they have reason to expect the dawn. They have been some time under the tuition of a master, whom mankind usually find to be a stern but good teacher—*Adversity*, and they

E

show a disposition to profit by the lessons. There is something in the prejudices of a Spaniard that is favorable to his advance, though it seems paradoxical to say so. He believes his country to be the first in the world—the soil of every good quality and excellence, and it has produced—*him*. He is courteous, he is honorable, because he believes courtesy and honor to be the characteristics of a Spaniard. As to his pride, he would, indeed, scarcely be a Spaniard if without it ; but when knowledge has pruned it of that rank exuberance which would overshadow all others, it rises into elevation of character and sentiment. Thus, I may say, prejudice is the mould on which his character is formed. Break it and hurl it away, and you will see what a well-shaped mind an intelligent Spaniard possesses.

One honorable trait of the clerical body here let me not omit. Unlike their brethren in the peninsula they have espoused warmly the constitutional cause. The present bishop was one of the deputies to the former *còrtes*. He is a man of high character, in general esteem. The island has two dioceses. Cuba was erected into an archbishoprick in 1804, and separated from the Havana, which has now a bishop of its own. The archbishoprick contains a cathedral, 22 parish churches and 5 auxiliaries. The diocese of the

Havana has a cathedral, erected in 1788, 45 parish churches, and 53 auxiliaries. The revenues of the bishop are about 60,000 dollars per annum. The usual income from benefices is from 2000 to 12,000 dollars.

The city is divided into 16 *quarteles,* and has 5 *barrio's,* or suburban parishes. It is surrounded by a strong wall with a ditch, and, independently of the forts *Morro* and *Punta,* has three others forming commanding outworks. The garrison at present is strong, being composed of six regiments of the line, four squadrons of dragoons and about 500 artillery of the line, between five and six thousand *regulars* in all. There are of *militia,* two battalions of foot and four squadrons of horse; 200 artillery; a regiment of free mulattoes and another of blacks, with 4480 foot volunteers, and 70 mounted ditto, (the former being raised in June last for the purpose of maintaining order) divided into 7 battalions, or 43 *compania's urbana's.*

Except the coloured militia, no other are kept constantly on foot, but usually exercise every Sunday in companies, and are reviewed in line once a year. The number of military in the other parts of the island is small, not above four or five thousand militia, and 70 regular artillery. The volunteer companies are, besides, established

E 2

in all the towns, but cannot be considered as a
field force, nor am I inclined to think, would the
discipline of the militia be found sufficient for *real*
practise in line. Taking a range of 30 miles
round the Havana, there were, in 1817, 20,577
white males from 15 to 60 years of age, including
the city population. Allowing for rank in life,
natural and accidental incapacity, perhaps, a third
should be deducted, and this will leave a recruiting total for the militia of 13,712 men. Allowing
still farther for the difficulties that would arise, in
case of an attack on the Havana, in concentrating
this species of force, or even the possibility of
drawing them from the necessary duties of home,
you will judge of the mass of military force that
could be employed.

The *compania's urbana's*, I mentioned, were
embodied in June last, for the preservation of
order. Their duty is to parade the streets in
detachments nightly, and this duty is unfortunately too necessary. Till of late assassinations
have been frightfully frequent and the numerous
advertisements in the *Diario's*, offering rewards
for *strayed* property, showed the laxity of the
police and the number of robberies. On the
18th of June last no less than *seven* people
(whites) were assassinated in the streets. A few
days before, the mayordomo of a nobleman had

been murdered in the *day time* while seated in his apartment. Indeed not a day passed without some instance of an attempt or commission of this most dastardly and horrid of crimes. In a petition preferred about this time to the captain-general, by the inhabitants of the Barrio *San Lazaro*, for a gate to be opened in the city wall from their suburb, it is mentioned as a leading reason for the request "that they may avoid the numerous *murders*, *robberies*, and *assaults* which they are liable to from the length of way from their *Barrio* to the *Alameda*, or public walk." These circumstances seem to have roused government to some little concern about the life of its subjects and the *compania's urbana's* were appointed for nightly patroles.

A mixed population, indolence without capital, a rage for gambling, and the light hold which crime takes upon consciences that can be washed clean by human hands, are to be regarded as the causes of this gross moral dereliction.* *Perhaps* if they were taught by their spiritual guides that it is sinful, and by their temporal that it is punishable, the character of the city would be different. I have frequently called to mind the national

* One hundred and fifty *wounded*, amongst the military only, were admitted into the hospital of *San Ambrosio* in 1818.

shudder which chilled 16 millions of people, when
the murder of the *Marr's* took place some years
ago in England; and as frequently reflected on
the anxious solicitude shown by all classes in that
happy island, (happy even with its radicals) to
discover and bring to merited punishment the
perpetrators of such crimes. But I cannot describe other countries properly if I am always
thinking of *England*.

My vague details have swelled my packet too
much. Let us rest a little here, for we have got
to stroll together over the city still farther.

LETTER IV.

Population of the Havana. Markets. Mode of living of the *Havanero's*. Description of a *Volante Corrida de Toros*, or Bull-fight. The *Alameda*. Females of the *Havana*. The Theatre. Havana *play-bill*. Critique on the Spanish drama. Gaming Houses. Dances. *Tertullia's*. *Catrès*.

In the year 1817, there were, within the walls of the Havana, 10,392 *white males* of all ages and 8,125 *white females*. The total coloured population, within the walls, was 12,738 males, and 13,214 females. Total of *intramural* population 44,319. This statement is exclusive of the regular garrison. The five *Barrio's* contain 7830 white males; 7831 white females; of coloured population, 6823 males and 7821 females. Total result 34,178 whites, 40,596 coloured people. Add to these the garrison, and the crews of the vessels that are daily entering the harbour, and you will conceive so many mouths must require well stocked markets.

In various parts of the city are large squares called *Plaza's*, and in these the markets are held.

Here you will find, about four in the morning,
an incredible number of white, black, and brown
Montero's, with the produce of the country twenty
miles round the town, brought in panniers across
mules and horses. It is surprising to see how
the poor animals are loaded with poultry, fruit,
maiz, malaxa (the stalk and leaf of the maiz cut
green, with which horses, &c. are fed) milk and
every species of vegetable, while, regardless of
the already sufficient load, the driver seats himself
between the panniers, smoking his çigar and
flourishing his whip. You never see a mule
drawing a cart without a driver astride on his
back, instead of easing the weight by riding (for
walking is out of the question) in the vehicle.
Notwithstanding this treatment the horses look
well, and will travel many leagues in the heat of
the sun at a shambling trot, with their burthens.
They are a small race, about the size of the road
hackney of England, and are tolerably docile, being usually rode without bridle or stirrups; a
nose-band or piece of rope is the common rein.
To finish this veterinary part of my epistle, let
me add, that the horses are seldom shod and *never*
curried, but are bathed regularly every morning.
    To return to market—the stalls (which pay a
duty to the municipality of a *real* per week, and
every loaded horse a *real* on entering the gates)

are well supplied with meat, fish, poultry (of which the turkies and quails are excellent) and every seasonable produce. The price of meat and bread is regulated by the *regidores*, who, previous to the re-establishment of the constitution, forestalled for themselves and friends the best of every thing. Meat is about a shilling English per pound, and the *Havanero*'s devour great quantities of it. They breakfast on meat, dine on meat, and sup on meat, with *buccanier* appetites. It it a patriotic appetite (if it be not *constitutional*) for immense herds of cattle range in the interior and also are reared in the *potrero's*, or breeding pens. But fresh meat, fish, poultry, and vegetables are all the island supplies itself with. The *tasago* or dried beef, the *bacalao* or dried fish (with which the negroes are fed) hams, rice, and all other eatables are supplied by foreigners. Flour to the amount of 80,000 barrels is annually imported ; though the soil of the island has been found capable of producing wheat. Near the towns of *Villa Clara* and *Santo Espiritu* to the eastward, good wheat is grown, as rice is likewise near *Las Guines*. There are some intelligent men in the island, not insensible to the advantages that would accrue from the enlarged cultivation of these necessaries of life, and

the retention of above two millions of dollars annually that are paid for them.

Luxury need not starve here, nor *does* it. The
tables of the rich are covered with a mob of dishes
and, after the grace (which I may call the *riot act*),
the surrounding authorities fall on them with
proper vigour. Dinner parties, however, are not
usual. When a festive occasion occurs in a family,
the entertainments commence with a breakfast
which is, in fact, an early dinner.

The *Cubano Cabalero* rises early and takes a
cup of chocolate as soon as risen. He then lights
his çigar and either strolls in his *patio*, or balconies,
or mounts his horse. At ten o'clock he breakfasts,
on fish, meat, soup, eggs and ham, with wine and
coffee. Before the company rise from table, a
little pan with live charcoal, is brought for every
one to light their çigars with. The females,
except in the upper ranks, *smoke* also. I can
scarcely draw the line precise here, for this incli-
nation of the females to turn into the neuter
gender, seems very great. I have seen the wives
and daughters of an *Official Real smoking in the
streets !* I have seen the wives and daughters
of *Abogado's*, *Physicians*, and *Alcalde's* smoking,
and yet, it is certainly true, what the gentlemen
tell you, that no *lady* smokes. This is a knotty

paradox ; but, if I remember right, the clown in
" The Winter's Tale" makes some observations
very illustrative of the point ; for my part, *I* am
not *clown* enough to attempt it.   Smoaking,
indeed, is so general that the people all look like
pictures of saints with glorified *halo's*.   It is said
the poor Mexicans were conquered so speedily
by their handful of invaders, from the consterna-
tion excited at the appearance of *Cortes'* sixteen
dragoons, they conceiving the man and horse
to be *one* animal.   If a body of Spaniards were
now to invade some *untobaccoed* Mexico, the man
and his çigar would certainly have the same fearful effect.   The *children* even smoke !   Little
creatures of five or six years old strut about with
their çigars ;   and, as parents dress the boys of
that age in long coats with little canes, they have
all the air of manhood, and only want whiskers
to make them appear as if set up to ridicule their
fathers.

But I rose rather abruptly from the breakfast
table.   What must we turn to next ?   That is a
question which pozes more than half the Havanero's very frequently.   Something or other must
be done—and the *volante* is ordered.   This vehicle has a body like the old French cabriolets,
set upon two enormous wheels, without springs,
but slung on leathers very easily.   It has a pair

of shafts, to the extreme end of which the horse
is attached, so that the wheels being at one end
and the horse at the other, bearing the weight
equally between them, the body swings with a
sort of palanquin effect. In the streets of the
Havana only *one* horse is allowed to this carriage,
and on it is mounted a stout negro, in a smart
livery, with long leather gaiters, made in the
form of Jack-boots, to which are attached a pair
of huge spurs, more calculated for an elephant
than a horse. In the country the driver usually
rides another than the shaft-horse, the extra one
being harnessed as an *outrigger*. In front of the
carriage a piece of dark blue woollen cloth is
spread, to keep off the dust and sun by day, and
the due by night. Immense numbers of these
vehicles crowd the streets, there being scarcely
any creditable white family without one ; and,
for those who cannot afford to keep one, there
are plenty of hackney *volantes* stationed in the
principal thoroughfares.

The heat of the day is the time for ceremonial
visiting, and, if it be a Sunday or a Saint's day,
you should drive round to make your bows. If
it be not, you must call only on your intimates—
balance yourself against the wall in a large arm
chair—take a bath—and—dress for dinner. This
period of renovation is at three o'clock, and sel-

dom lasts above an hour, for, like all foreigners,
the Spaniards do not drink wine after dinner.
Before they rise from table the little charcoal pan
again makes its appearance.   Coffee ensues.
The conversation gradually relaxes, and each re-
tires to take his *siesta.*   In less than an hour all
are again in motion.   The *volante* is ordered ;
perhaps there is a *corrida de toros*, or bull-fight,
and thither the Havana world flock.   These
entertainments take place only occasionally, and
are held in a large wooden circular building
without the walls.   It is a most difficult thing to
get entrance, so great is the attraction, especially
if the bulls are " *todos de muerte*"—*all to be
killed*, and to be *stuck with fireworks.*   The produce is usually between 2000 and 3000 dollars.

If there is no *corrida*, you will proceed to the
alameda, or public walk, a long regular grove,
with a broad carriage way and footpaths and seats
on each side.   It lies without the walls, at the
farther extremity, having a military hospital and
the *barracones*, or guard houses where the fresh
imported negroes are lodged for sale.   Thus a
stranger on casting his eye along, while the road
way is filled with gay *volantes* and loungers, may
see at once the three peculiarities of a West India
island.—A luxurious population, slavery and the
yellow fever !

It is really an agreeable scene to view on *grand* days this gay concourse. The *capacete* (or dark woollen cloth in front of the *volante*) is removed on these occasions, and the fair *cubana's* indulge the crowd with an unclouded view of their persons seated on these whirling thrones. Bright dark eyes in profusion are seen quick glancing from passing *volantes*, and these are unshaded by ringlet or bonnet, the hair being divided *à la Greque* and always uncovered. It is only while at church that the fair one wears her *mantilla* or veil, thrown over the head and shoulders, and held more or less close over her face according to the state of her devotion. On those occasions also, they dress in black, according to the old Spanish fashion, but at other times, their attire is light and airy, between English and French, but more inclining to the latter. In person they are generally well-made, and in the upper ranks, fair. The manners of these latter are lively and agreeable, and though custom sanctions a broader cast of expression on subjects which an English lady either avoids or blushes at, yet they are, I fully believe, unimpeached as faithful wives and dutiful daughters. The best proof of this belief is, that every one inclines to matrimony. The education of females is a point now fully attended to. French, music, geography and history are taught in all respectable families. There are no *Hannah More's* here, and therefore *Latin* is left to the gentlemen.

There is one symptom here of good sense in the men and virtue in the women—*jealousy* seems extinct. The females range at full liberty, and sit at their windows gazing on the passengers without fear of being *locked up!* neither *duena*, nor *lattice* have I seen in the house of a husband, and, what are still worse tidings to the lovers of romance, not a *serenade* have I heard.

Of the *lower* order of white females I wish I could speak complimentary. The fact is, they want *education*, and wanting that, they want every thing. Their habits are dirty, their minds and manners indolent. You will see female friends at the doors of their houses in the cool of the evening examining the contents of each others heads, but not *intellectually*. They seem not to have the least idea that there is any thing disgusting in it. I am inclined to believe that the 274 foundlings taken to the hospital at the Havana last year, must be placed to the account of this class.

This is a digression, but a natural one. We will not, however, return to the *alameda*, for it is time to go to the *theatre*, if there is an *opera* performed ; if there is only a " *comedia famosa*"

we will leave the house to the rabble. It is
usual to take a box for the season, or a certain
length of time—three or four months, and if you
do not, you will get no box seat. You pay four
reales for your admission at the outward door,
and afterwards an additional sum according to
the part of the house, or nature of the accommo-
dation you choose. The company is tolerable,
and the house convenient, though not large. It
is only *fully* lighted on grand nights, which circumstance is always advertised, as is the *programme* of the piece, as—" This evening will be
" presented to the illustrious and respectable
" people of the *Havana*, the famous and much-
" admired comedy entitled ' *El Triunfo del Ave
" Maria*,' in which *Senor Garcia* will perform
" the part of a *Graciozo*, who delivers many truly
" agreeable and witty speeches, as will the *Senora
" Gamborino* the character of a *Graciosa*, whose
" diverting observations and smart speeches
" will give great delight to the audience. The
" comedy will be adorned by appropriate dresses
" and scenes, amongst others the march of the
" heroic Spanish army to attack the infidels,
" with suitable warlike accompaniments—the
" Spanish hero on horseback—the moorish chief-
" tain advancing to challenge the Spaniards, when
" the Spanish conqueror with the assistance of the

"*Ave Maria* will cut off the head of the moor;—
" with many other agreeable and surprising inci-
" dents. After this will be performed the excel-
" lent and much admired piece called *The re-*
" *establishment of the constitution*, "written by an
" eminent patriot, where will be seen the ceremo-
" ny of laying the *lapida* of our most glorious
" constitution. Also will be seen the portraits of
" those Spanish heroes, *Quiroga* and *Riego*, and a
" procession of *Alcalde's* and other authorities.
" The Theatre will be illuminated with perfect
" brilliancy so as to afford this most respectable
" public every satisfaction."—I have seen a Spanish work, published in London the beginning of
this year, which says the English Theatre is in a
state of *semi-barbarism*. I will not say the same,
exactly, of the Spanish Theatre, but there certainly is much wildness (*poetic* if you please) in their
dramatic compositions. Of their modern drama
little can be said; there is a playfulness in their
dialogue but nothing of *character*, which I take
to be the main requisite. Their old writers are
full of fanciful expression; but their heroes, their
gracioso's and their ladies, only vary in names;
they are the same beings carried through a series
of plots. I think *Moreto* has shewn more discrimi-
nation and delicate touch in respect to character
than most of the former writers. His " *Primera*

F

es la Honra" has these qualities with much natural growth of sentiment, less choaked by metaphoric flowers than usual. The *saynete's*, or *entertainments* of the Spaniards have a good deal of spirit in their dialogues—Much of the *gracioso* character, which is *quip* and *legerite ;* but the higher order of pieces are stilted and bombastic, full of strange anachronisms, tedious speeches and walking gentlemen. As to the aforesaid *programme* and the *Havana* taste, I am restricted from saying more, because I just recollect I saw " *Timour the Tartar*," *Madame Sacchi*, and an *elephant* in a christmas *pantomime* on the boards of a London Theatre-royal.

There is yet a time-killing resource if the Theatre is not attractive. A short distance beyond the walls of the Havana are situated two or three large elegant houses with spacious saloons and painted decorations, for I forgot to tell you that the apartments of the houses are whitewashed half-way from the cieling and painted below in compartments in a very gay stile. A lamp hangs from the centre—A sofa, little tables fitted to the corners and ranges of rather ordinary chairs, compose the whole of the usual fitting up of apartments. The houses I allude to are, however, more splendid in their furniture. They are the residences of individuals who light them up nightly

and throw open the doors to the public. Any
white person may enter without invitation and
there he or she will find music for dancing, and
tables for playing *monte*, the favorite game of the
Cubano's. In point of fact these are *gaming-
houses* where the owner makes his profit by the
tables. So little does opinion incline against
them, that they are held by persons who are in,
otherwise, respectable life, and fathers of families
frequent them with their wives and daughters, so
that you will really find *good company* there.

You have probably heard that dancing is a favorite *West India* amusement. It is not so much
the *rage* here as in the English islands, but still
it is a favorite. The minuet (the proper dance
of the climate) keeps a place here though nearly
banished the other world. The *Fandango* is the
truly national one and you may frequently see it
performed as you pass the houses in the evening.

The *Tertullia* is the Spanish *rout*, conducted,
however, with due gravity and order. The Havana can supply many room fulls of agreeable
and pretty women and rational gentlemenly men ;
but there is a formal air in the good breeding of
the latter very *old-schoolish*. When a well-bred
caballero takes leave after a visit he will make you
a bow of a most correct right angle, another,

when half way to the door, and a third he turns
round to make as he touches the threshold. All
this is very well, it looks courteous and stately
and would impress one with a high notion of habitual drawing-room manners, if the gentleman
had not been, all the time of his visit, spitting
round his chair so as to nearly turn your sto-
mach.

I am beginning to be censorious again. The
fact is I am tired of my pleasurable tour, and it
is now high time to think of repose.

The bed most commonly used is merely a cross-
legged frame of wood, on which is stretched a
piece of canvas. On this are laid a pair of thin
sheets between which you extend yourself, while
a slender framework upholds a net which closes
all round you to exclude the *mosquitoes*. This is
called a *Catre*. It requires a little habit to recon-
cile your bones to its use, but its freshness will
certainly induce you to change your mattrass for
it.

On this dormitory (if there are neither scorpions nor lizards, nor *arana peluda's*, " or large
hairy spiders whose bite is venemous" nor cock-
roaches, under my pillow) I can lay myself down
with much satisfaction, especially, if, on closing
my eyes upon the scenes I have described to you,

I am borne back in visions to "that precious stone
set in the silver sea" whose murmuring population only require to be placed out of it for a space,
to regard it as it is—the land of good sense, refinement, rational enjoyment, and, let me empha-
tically add, *rational liberty.*

LETTER V.

Foundation of the Havana; progress of its commerce ; opening
of its port to a national trade ; other ports of Cuba so privileged. Effects of this measure on the revenue of the
island. Rapid advance of Matanzas. National monopoly
destroyed, and free commerce conceded to the ports of
Havana, Cuba, Trinidad and Matanzas. Effects of the same.
Revenue; aid supplied by it to other governments. Exports
of the island; imports. Ports of Baracoa and Mariel opened.
Recent difficulties of the treasury of the island ; their causes.
Resources; disposition of the government to encrease them.
New settlements on the island; account of their progress and
condition. Funds for promoting them and other institutions.

It is commerce which has made the *Havana*
what it is, and upon its increase or decline de-
pends the peopling of the vast tracts of this island
which have lain for centuries untrod. Cuba had
been settled for many years before its importance
and value were understood, even by the settlers.
Diego Velasquez, when he founded the Havana
in 1515, thought only of rendering it a stepping-
stone to Mexico, and a depot for military adventurers. The tide of population rolled on to the

costa firme as the grand scene of speculation, occasionally touching at, or being repelled back to,
this port from the shores of New Spain and
Florida.   In 1576, however, it appears to have
become a place worth attending to, for, in that year,
the Franciscans founded a convent of their order
in the Havana, and were followed, two years
after, by the Dominicans.   Another proof of its
rising importance is, that it was twice sacked by
the English and French about the same period.
It was not walled round till 1633, when the captain-generalship of the island having been annexed
to the government of the city, it became the point
of concentration for commerce, the galleons making it their regular port of entry.   This commerce, however, (carried on solely by galleons
and register ships) remained long so trifling and
unproductive, that the expences of government
were nearly entirely borne by the treasury of
Mexico, eighteen hundred dollars being annually
remitted for that purpose.   The ports of this
island, which are, for the most part, capable of
containing ships to any amount of number or
burthen, were suffered to lie unused, on the
futile principle of exclusive monopoly.   It was
not till 1778 that Spain saw the impolicy of such
restriction, but, as if awoke in the dark, she acted
with fear and caution, opening only a few of the

ports of this island to an intercourse with the peninsula. These were the *Havana, Cuba, Trinidad*, and *Batabanò*. The same privilege was subsequently granted to other ports; and, as the dates of these grants afford a mean of judging of the local advance of various parts of the island and the course which the flow of population has taken, I shall give them here—

NUEVITAS (on the north coast, in the jurisdiction of Puerto Principe, 170 leagues east of the Havana) 5th August, 1784.

MATANZAS (on the north coast, 22 leagues east of the Havana) 3d December, 1793.

SAN JUAN DE LOS REMEDIOS (on the north coast, 90 leagues east of the Havana) 14th May, 1796.

BARACOA (on the north east coast 324 leagues from the Havana, and 78 from Cuba) 21st July, 1803.

MANZANILLO (on the south coast, in the jurisdiction of Bayamo, 218 leagues from Havana) 21st July, 1803.

EL GOLETO (on the south coast, in the jurisdiction of *Santo Espiritu*, 114 leagues from the Havana) 21st July, 1803.

Previous to the year 1778 (when the first

named ports were partially liberated) the export
of the staple commodity, sugar, was little more
than 200,000 quintals, equal to 12,500 English
hogsheads.* The worst soil in the West Indies
produces more than a hogshead of 16 cwt. from
every two acres, and, therefore, taking even this
minimum, it would seem that only 25,000 acres
cultivated with sugar, out of the many millions
which the island contains. But the advantages
accruing to agriculture and trade were soon observable, and that we may more clearly note
them, it will be proper here to notice the finan-
cial arrangement of the island, from the results of
which we must estimate its progress.

The island is divided into three *Intendancies* or
finance governments—*Havana, Cuba,* and *Puerto
Principe,* the Intendant of the first being the
Superintendante general de hacienda publica and
having the entire administration of the revenue.

---

* A *quintal* is equal to a *cwt.* Four *arroba's* make a *quintal*
and every *caxa,* or box of Spanish sugar contains from 16 to 20
arroba's. The *caxa* is 45 inches long, and 22½ inches broad.
There is no rule as to the height, that depending on the size of
the boards. This accounts for the variation as to contents. The
caxas themselves usually weigh from 35 to 70℔ each. In the
bocois of melasses there is the same inequality, there being from
16 to 20 barrels in each *bocoy;* the barrel containing 10 *frasco's*
or 30 *quartillo's* or pints.

A pipe of rum contains 180 *frasco's* or 67½ gallons. Jamaica
exported 73,304 hogsheads of sugar in 1774.

Subordinate to these *Indendancies* are ten subaltern districts, or *Administraciones terorerias,* under the management of *Subdelegado's.* These have the care of the interior revenue (which previous to the year 1703 was not worth collecting) and have *Administradores* stationed throughout the districts for the purposes of collection. Every habilitated port has its *Subdelegado,* likewise subject to the *Intendente* of his district.

There are no perfect returns of the produce of the ten *Administraciones* till 1762; the records being *partially* destroyed by moths (edax archivorum) up to that year, and *entirely* so previous to 1735. In the former year (1762) the total produce of these districts was 23,040 dollars, or £5184. In 1778 they produced 158,624 or £35,690. Particular instances show the advance more strongly. The town of *Matanzas* had a *Subdelegado* appointed in 1756. Its situation, on the north coast, 22 leagues from Havana, looking down the gulf of Florida, possessing a good harbour and a fertile tract of country around it, seemed peculiarly favourable to commerce. But in 1762 it produced in revenue the paltry item of 74 dollars, or £16 . 13s. !! Though not habilitated till 1793, yet its proximity to the Havana occasioned its participation in commercial extension, and in 1780 its revenue from interior

duties produced 7167 dollars, or £1612 . 11 . 6;
one hundred times its former produce. In 1794
(being the end of the first year of its habilitation)
the duties on entry amounted to 812 dollars, or
£182 . 14, and its internal duties to 9091 dollars,
or £2045 . 9 . 6; being together £2228 . 3 . 6.
In 1818 this same Matanzas contributed in revenue a total of 249,023 dollars, being £56,030,
having in the space of 56 years encreased the
produce of its imposts nearly *four thousand fold!**
The total amount of the ten districts from internal duties was, in 1818, 618,036 dollars, or
£139,058.

You will observe that these ten districts do not
include the Havana, and that the duties, the
amount of which I have stated, are laid on *internal*
dealings. Their amount, therefore, is only evidence
of the progrss of population and domestic trade ;
and it gives these results, that little more than a
century ago, the first was not sufficiently numerous and concentrated, or the second of sufficient
value to bear imposts ; and that, since these were

* This port during the last year (1819) received 268 vessels,
and had 265 clear out, having been priviledged as a free port in
1809. The export of sugar was, 42,279 *caxas ;* of coffee, 47,941
arroba's. Five thousand four hundred and forty-seven negroes
were imported from Africa to this place during the same period.
Total produce of imports 308,419 dollars.

laid, the advance of population and internal trade
has been in rapid progress. No one can doubt
that these benefits have arisen from a change of
system, from the shackles of monopoly being broken and commerce allowed the range it requires.
But the decree of 1778 did not give such scope.
A restriction of intercourse to Spain, and in
Spanish bottoms was little suited to the craving
nature of trade, and the political circumstances of
the mother country, made even that privilege almost nugatory. In thirty years Cuba had little
more than trebled her produce of sugar. It is
true she had raised a new and highly productive
staple—coffee; that the tobacco she cultivated
was the first in the market; and that nearly
20,000 arroba's of wax were exported annually.
But notwithstanding these additional products of
her soil and industry, still, previous to the admission of foreign vessels into her ports, the total
amount of her exports was not much above
5,000,000 dollars, or £1,000,000,* while the
revenue raised upon this, the return cargoes and
internal duties did not suffice, by nearly a million
and a half of dollars, for the payment of government expences.

The cure for these evils was at last attempted,

---

* Jamaica in 1774 exported above the value of £2,000,000.

and in 1809 the ports of the Havana, Cuba, Trinidad, and Matanzas were thrown open to the vessels
of all nations and the speculative industry of the
world.   Since that period a considerable advance
has been made towards improvement in every
way.   Above eleven hundred ships of all flags
now enter annually the port of Havana.   So
greatly has the cultivation of coffee encreased that
it is estimated 25,000,000 dollars are vested in
that branch, in the province of Havana.   About
double that sum is the amount, which the best informed people judge, has been added to the employed capital of the island within the few years
that a free trade has been conceded to it.   Con-
current with the advance of agriculture and
commerce has been that of the revenue which
annually amounts to above four millions of dollars; the statement for the year ending 31st
December 1819 giving 4,104,568.   In 1818 the
receipts amounted to 3,793,914 dollars, which
added to 573,668 dollars, the balance of 1817,
gives a total of 4,366,982 dollars.   The expenditure for 1818 was 3,686,993 dollars, leaving a
surplus of 679,989 dollars for the service of 1819.
During this last year the receipts, as I have mentioned, were 4,104,568 dollars, which with the balance of 1818, afford 4,784,557 dollars.   The expenditure for 1819 was 3,847,890 dollars, leaving a

balance of 936,667 dollars carried to the account
of the current year 1820.

When from the expenditure of the island you
have deducted 469,370 dollars remitted to the
Floridas for their support (for you are aware these
provinces form part of this captain-generalship);
nearly 100,000 to Santo Domingo and the emigrants from it; about a million and a half to the
regulars in garrison and the royal marine, exclusive of militia expences; 25,377 dollars to *Puerto-
Rico* and nearly 400,000 to support the royal
causes in S. America; you may form an estimate
of the advantages which a free trade has conferred
on this island. The Havana alone in 1819 exported—

192,743 boxes of sugar $\left\{\begin{array}{c}\text{equal to}\\\text{about}\end{array}\right\}$ 850,000 cwt.

642,716 arroba's of coffee . .   160,679 cwt.

30,845 bocois of melasses . . 1,974,000 gallons

2,830 pipes of rum . . .   191,017 gallons

19,373 arroba's of wax . .   4,843 cwt.

The value of these may be estimated at about
nine millions of dollars, or more than two millions
of pounds sterling.—From the port of Matanzas
(next in point of commerce to that of the Havana)
were exported in 1819—

*14,760 boxes of sugar . . .   60,000 cwt.

35,198 arroba's of coffee . .   8,799 cwt.

8,216 bocois of melasses . . 525,804 gallons

The value of these exports may be computed to be a million of dollars. The exports of the port of *Cuba* amount to nearly the same sum, judging from the produce of its imports, for want of the returns of its commerce. *Trinidad*, by the same mode of calculation, exported in value about two hundred thousand dollars. The port of *Baracoa* was in August 1815 allowed to receive four or five foreign vessels† with articles of first necessity, and in December 1816 entirely laid open, but its commerce is very inconsiderable, notwithstanding that the duties imposed are only half of those levied at the Havana. *Mariel*, likewise, an excellent port some leagues to the west of the Havana, has been habilitated by royal order of 29th February 1820. Its export, however, (to the amount of nearly 50,000 boxes of sugar, besides coffee &c.) has hitherto been sent to the Havana and cleared out from thence. From this summary review, therefore, it would appear that the value

* There were also 27,519 boxes of sugar ; 12743 arroba's of coffee, and 139 hocois of melasses cleared out for other ports of the island ; but this is chiefly included in the Havana export.

† Such are the terms of the royal decree of habilitation !

of exports from the island of Cuba, in sugar, coffee, wax, rum and melasses, amounts to about 11,200,000 dollars, or £2,520,000.

In addition to this the island exports *tobacco* to the amount of nearly two millions of dollars; *hides* to the value of 80,000 dollars, and preserved fruits, cabinet wood, honey, &c. amounting to 150,000 dollars. Thus the export of produce may be estimated at 13,230,000 dollars, or £2,976,750.

On the other hand, the island imports flour, wine, and dry provisions to the amount of 2,500,000 dollars; lumber to the value of 700,000 dollars, and manufactured goods to that of 6,000,000 dollars; in all 9,200,000 dollars, or £2,070,000. You will observe that I have not considered the slave trade, the most profitable of all, and which has been in full vigour during the period from which this calculation has been made. At the lowest estimate, slaves to the value of 5,000,000 dollars have been brought to the island during the last year. I am very much inclined to believe that the great proportion of capital employed in this traffic was *foreign*, and consequently the profits cannot be credited entirely to the island. Taking, however, the value of the imported slaves into the general estimate, the total imports would be 14,200,000 dollars, or £3,195,000.

Thus far has the commerce of the Havana advanced in the short period of eleven years, though
considerably harassed by the armed cruisers of
the dissident provinces of Spanish America and
feeling, in common with the world at large, the
political quakes of Europe. Of late, indeed,
(that is, within the last nine months) commerce
has slackened sensibly. The exhausted state of
the mother country, the shaken credit of the united states and the pressure of restrictive systems
which Europe has not yet abandoned, have
affected the exports of the island and consequently
the revenue derived from them. In consequence
of these circumstances and their visible effects, the
government here on the 19th of June last (1820)
were obliged to adjust their imposts to the ne-
cessities of the time. The reasons given for new-
modelling the duties are—" the decay of maritime
" trade—the small entry of vessels—the lessened
" exportation of produce* the lowering of its
" value, particularly of rum and melasses which
" scarcely pay their transport to a place of ship-
" ment, and this also occurring at a time *when a*
" *traffic most essential to the cultivation of the plant-*

* Above 10,000 boxes of sugar more were exported in the first
seven months of 1818 than the same period of 1819, and there
were nearly 200,000 arrobas of coffee excess in that time above
the export of 1819.

G

" *ations* is put an end to."* The consequence has
been that the revenue has materially suffered,
when its expences are encreased by the augmentation of the garrison and the assistance required
by the mother country for the support of its cause
on the *Terra firma* of America. When the constitution was re-established a few months back the
payment of imposts was withstood by nearly every
class of people here, conceiving that the abrogation of arbitrary power carried with it every particle of its system. So strongly impressed, or rather
so weak, were the people on this point that they

---

* This is the language of the government, and is a prognostic
of the spirit with which we must expect the abolition laws will be
administered.

A *near relation* of *one* of the Spanish commissioners for the
abolition of the slave trade, thus expresses himself in a pamphlet
just published here in defence of the conduct of the *other* commissioner, the *intendant* of the island.

" The English cabinet, *the implacable enemy of the property
of other countries,* had long *brooded over a design to ruin this
island,* a favourite object of its ambition ever since the malignant
eloquence of Sheridan compared it to a young giant. That cabinet, subverting the principles of commerce, as if displeased at
the national tendency, took up the beautiful and philanthropic
philosophy of the estimable Wilberforce; and with its usual
course of policy, *forced* from our government, then a mere
shadow, the *treaty,* which, *ruinous* as it is to this island, is not
yet so prejudicial as *humiliating* and *odious* in the manner of
abolishing the slave trade."

absolutely shook off every sort of restraint, and at
the moment I am now penning this letter (five
months after the re-establishment of constitutional
sway) there is scarcely an official character in the
island who has courage to act. The treasury is
dry—*literally speaking*, the laws sleep—self-will
only reigns and nothing is seen but the most
audacious violations of public order—nothing
heard in the tribunals but the quarrels of their
members and the sneers of the crowd. The fact
is, that *liberty* is a word not hitherto to be found
in the Spanish dictionary, and the people do not
comprehend it. Every one, therefore, interprets it
as he pleases, some deriving it from the *French*,
some from the *English*, and very many from the
Tartarian. A little time, an energetic government, and a further reform in the administration
of justice, will set all to rights; for there are not
wanting men of sense in this city, and the encouragement of these and the repression of that
absorbent spirit of freedom which takes all and
gives none (too common at present) will effect a
real and salutary reform.

Besides this stagnancy of payment, there are
other causes of the present embarrassment of the
treasury of the island, viz. the cessation of several
imposts which had been in the former æra declared
unconstitutional by the còrtes. The *estanco* or royal

monopoly of tobacco, the sale of offices, and the
additional imposts on *pulperia's* or provision-
shops, are thus circumstanced. The *alcabala* or
sale duty upon slaves has also terminated. Add
to these, losses which the revenue frequently suffers by the failure of merchants and the tardiness
of *hacendado's*, renters of public estates and con-
tractors. Several heavy failures have occurred
within the last year; and, it may be presumed,
(since the termination of the slave trade will
shut up the most profitable source of wealth to
many) that others will follow. But the resources are great and it is only necessary to stop the
drain upon them, which the contest between
Spain and her colonies is causing, to fill to reple-
tion the local channels of irrigation which a pa-
ternal and wise government ought to form for
them.

I must candidly avow that for some years past
government has been by no means inattentive to
the advancement of the island and the nurture of
its population. For the latter purpose a royal
decree was issued in October, 1817, which directed
lands on various parts of the northern and southern
coasts to be appropriated to such white persons
as might be induced to settle on them. A fund
has been raised by a provisional duty of six dollars on every *male* slave imported from Africa.

It commenced 10th of February 1818, and down to the 30th November 1819 had produced 106,130 dollars. From this fund the government engages to pay to every *catholic* white person who may emigrate hither, the sum of three reales (1s. 8¼d.) per day to each adult, and the half of that sum to those under fifteen years of age, during the first two months after their arrival : one dollar per league, for travelling expences, from the port of their disembarkation to the spot assigned them for residence, to each adult, and four reales to every minor as described. The parts of the island se‑lected for the establishment for such as may be tempted to settle are, *Nuevitas* on the N. coast ; *Guantanamo* on the eastern (known to the English by the name of *Walthenam*, or *Cumberland harbour*); a tract of six leagues square, contiguous to the bay of *Jagua* on the N. coast, and another of about four leagues and a half, called Santo Domingo, nearly four leagues from the north coast, ten leagues west of *Villa Clara*, and seventy from the Havana.

Every white person above the age of eighteen, if he arrives at *Nuevitas* before April 1821, re‑ceives in absolute propriety a *caballeria* of land (32 acres), with a stipulation that he must com‑mence its cultivation within six months and get the half of it, at least, into a productive state within two years. Nearly four hundred persons have at different times since the publication of this grant, availed themselves of its presumed benefit ; but, whether from indolence, or insuperable difficulty, discouragement has arisen and the new settlement is gradually wearing away.*

At the bay of *Guantanamo* and *Santo Domingo* those who present themselves between January 1820 and December 1821, are offered the same privileges. After the ultimate periods given by the grants of *Nuevitas* and the two last named settlements, the *gift* of lands will cease and those, then unappropriated, will be offered on terms of remuneration ; the first year after the termination of the period of gift, at the rate of one hundred dollars for every caballeria of land ; the second year at one hundred and twenty-five dollars ; with a progressive addition of twenty-five dollars every year till the expiration of ten years. The port of *Guantanamo* has also recently been habilitated and an additional impost of two per cent (beyond the current duties) laid on export produce, to pay for the erection of a battery to defend the port, and also for a custom-house and beacon.

---

* According to a late report by a person opposed to government, and who uses it as a ground of accusation, not more than thirty or forty persons were remaining in June, 1817. The port will only admit ships of small burthen.

There are already seventy-eight plantations in the vicinity and a subaltern factory of tobacco was established there ; while the excellence of the bay and its admirable situation for commerce, can scarcely fail to cause its rapid increase.

The settlement at *Santo Domingo* does not possess these advantages. It is true that it is situated amidst the corn fields of Cuba, wheat being cultivated there with success and the low lands capable of producing tobacco ; while its higher portions are stocked with cedar, mahogany and *àcana* (a wood used for furniture). But the river *Zagua*, which runs through it, forms, by its winding, a course of seven leagues to the sea, or the place of embarkation and to this last spot only vessels of small burden can approach. These difficulties will probably prevent its attaining any great height.

On the shore of the bay of *Jagua*, a retired officer of the regiment of *Luisiana* lieutenant colonel *D. Louis de Clouvet* has obtained a grant of one hundred *caballerias* of land and has settled there with forty families of Spanish colonists from Luisiana. Within two years two hundred and forty one persons have settled there. Thirty dollars per head are allowed by the government for every person coming from *Luisiana*, or the *United States* and sixty dollars for each one proceeding from Europe.

For the first six months they are to receive $3\frac{1}{2}$
reales per day and may import every article of
necessity free of duty for five years, that is till
1824. The inhabitants of the respective settlements are precluded from selling their grants till
the expiration of five years after possession.

Besides the attempt to encrease the *amount* of
white population, the government have endea-
vored to improve its *quality*. The establishment
of schools throughout the island has been actively
promoted by the *economical society* of the *Havana*,
and for this and other patriotic purposes a royal
order, in August 1818, granted a deduction of
three per cent, on certain branches of the revenue,
to be paid to the treasurer of the society. Thirty
one thousand nine hundred and twenty dollars
had been so paid in the first ten months ; between
forty and fifty thousand dollars per annum. A
nautical school has also been established within
the last three years, and a duty of two *reales*, on
every *bocay* of melasses exported from this harbour, granted for its support. The produce is
between three and four thousand dollars per
annum. A professorship of anatomy and of
chemistry—A school for painting and lectureship
or political œconomy have also been established
under the patronage of the government. But
time and enlarged intercourse with the ideas of

other nations who are past infancy, are wanting to form the recipiency of mind that will render these institutions thoroughly available. At present I can only say that a medical man gravely advises his patients to *perspire four shirts*, or to remain in the bath during three *paternosters* and an *ave maria* : that the priests are as fat and thriving as they could have been in the 15th century ; that a Jew dare not for his life appear in the island ; that *cockpits* have been found sufficiently valuable to become objects of royal monopoly and that above 10,000 packs of cards are annually imported !!

LETTER VI.

THE country round the Havana, within a circuit of ten miles, is comparatively barren; dis-
forested, drained and neglected. The sun and
the rains beating for above a century on the bald
surface of the earth have, alternately, washed and
desiccated the soil.   Here and there, in the
shaded vallies, pieces of culture are seen, sown
with maiz, the stalk and grain of which afford
food for cattle. The roads are mere tracks or
gullies worn free of soil by the rains, traversing
the naked rock and partaking of all its rugged-
ness. Convenience has traced them out in the

first instance, and use has, in some degree, worked
them into form. By public regulation the lines
of communication between the towns must be 16
yards in breadth ; that is, no house, fence, or en-
closure must be raised near these tracks, (which
we will call roads) so as to diminish that breadth,
where it naturally exists; for in some parts the
track is pent up between the rocks to a much less
distance. The roads into the interior cross the
mountains by some very perilous ascents, which
will only admit horses and mules. The number
of small rivers, also, which cross the island (rising
in the mountains and flowing on each side, north
and south to the sea) frequently impede travellers
in the rainy season, though bridges both of stone
and wood are usually placed over them. For the
construction and maintenance of these and the
better regulation of the roads, the government, in
September 1818, instituted a tax of four dollars
per head on every male slave imported from
Africa. But the natural difficulties of the roads
(common to all tropical countries) are trifling,
compared to the obstructions and dangers arising
from the black and white robbers which infest
them. Woe to the solitary unarmed traveller, if
such an unadvised inexperienced being should
venture himself amidst the rugged *sierra's* of the
interior !

In pursuing the route inland from the Havana you meet with scarcely any thing that attracts notice for the first two leagues. On crossing the harbour you land at a small town called *Regla*, situated on the swampy shore, a mile and a half from the city. It is the *Rotherhithe* or *Blackwall* of the Havana, with all the miry loathsomeness of a Spanish suburb. Two miles from this, on the further side of a rocky eminence, is the town of *Guanabacoa*, the summer resort of the *Havanero's*. The appearance of this and, indeed, of all the interior towns of the island, is something like a ruined English village, in point of buildings. The houses, exteriorly, have the precise look of *barns* and *mud cottages*, while the masses of rugged rock, interspersed amongst them, and upon which they are built, gives an air of devastation to the whole town. Pavement or footpath, there are none, nor, indeed, would it be an easy task to level the huge blocks spread through the streets or to fill up the cavities between them. In this town there are several mineral springs and public baths, much frequented in the summer season.

The road to Matanzas (the most frequented from the Havana) runs through this town; the distance is twenty leagues. For the first twelve miles there is scarcely any ascent ; the country is evel and open, very thinly spread with huts and

cultivated tracts. Those who reside on them are
white people, some of whom possess a slave or
two, and breed pigs and poultry, keep cows to
supply the neighbouring towns with milk, and
raise *muniato's*, *yucas*, garlic, *tomate's*, melons,
calabashes, oranges, *mameyes*, *sapote's* &c for the
markets of the Havana. On approaching these
solitary residences, which only impress one with
more dreary ideas, the yells of dogs and naked
children, prove how singular a sight a stranger is.
As to hospitality, it is not to be expected or desired. There are, indeed, on this route to Matanzas, two *posada's* or *hedge-inns*, but they are not
calculated to afford either entertainment or security to one above the rank of a drover. The
usual mode of travelling is to proceed with one
pair of horses, or mules, to your *volante*, and
another following it, and to push on as fast as
practicable. It is wonderful to see the adroitness
with which these animals move over the rugged
roads, and the unwearied patience with which they
toil on beneath a burning sun. For the draught
of produce, oxen only are employed; but the
carbonero's, or *charcoal burners* and the suppliers
of the markets, who frequently dwell in situations
unsuitable for carriages, load their respective
articles on the backs of mules, long cavalcades of
which one frequently meets on the road.

The first *ingenio*, or sugar plantation, you come to, on the road to Matanzas by *Guanabo*, is nearly five leagues from the Havana, one from the town of *Guanabo*, and about the same distance from the sea. This last mentioned town is a poor miserable place with a church and about twenty thatched huts, (or houses if you will) inhabited by petty farmers of maiz and market produce. The population consists of about one hundred and twenty whites, and nearly the same number of negroes. Half a league from hence commences the *sierra* or mountainous ridge, which crosses the island in a south easterly direction; forming a natural barrier, indented with some very difficult passes. To the N. E. and S. W of this lie many *ingenio's* and on its gentlest ascents are many *potrero's*, or breeding pens, where vast numbers of hogs, black cattle and horses are reared. Some of these *potrero's* contain above a thousand acres, though, in the remoter parts of the island, there are some properties devoted to this purpose, nearly two or three leagues square. The *ingenio's*, in general, contain about 600 or 700 acres annually cropt.

Proceeding eastward about two leagues from *Guanabo*, you arrive at a river formed by the junction of the *Giguia* and the *Jaruco*. At this point a small population has collected and wharfs are raised on the banks of the river (about a league

from the sea) to which small vessels can work up
to load produce. There are many fine estates in
the neighbourhood; the *ingenio's* de Giguiabo ;
de Jauregui ; Rioblanco de Penalver, and a caffetal belonging to the *Conde de Loreto*, more particularly so.

The town of *Rio Blanco* is but a short distance
from this; for here every assemblage of huts, with
a church in the midst of them, is a *town*. But, in
traversing this space, a human habitation is like
manna in the wilderness, and we naturally mag-
nify what is rare and unexpected. The *Partido
de Santa Cruz*, upon which we next enter, is well
covered with *potero's* and *estancia's** in which
some tobacco is cultivated.

The river *Santa Cruz* allows of small vessels
entering a few miles up and loading, to facilitate
which wharfs are erected on its banks.

The small town of *Gibacoa* is about two leagues
farther east. It has a church and a scanty population ; lying in a valley, through which flows a
rivulet that admits boats to carry the wood cut
in the neighbouring hills, which nearly surround
the town, to the place of embarkation on the
coast.

* An *estancia* is a cultivated piece of land not devoted to the
produce of sugar or coffee.

Formerly the island carried on a tolerable trade in wood, of which it produces almost every tropical variety   Of these the *Cedro ; Coaba ; Pino ; Acana ; Chicatron ; Sabicu ; Jobo ; Quiebrahacha*, or iron wood; *Jocuma de corazon ; Roble,* or *Oak ; Guallo* and *Frigolillo* (much used for joists and supporters in the construction of houses) ; *elocuge* and *la Lebisa* (for hen coops and boarding); the *Dagame* (for axle trees); the *Guira* (for yokes and handles of ploughs) ; the *Cuagani* (for the frames of carts and waggons); are abundant. About the year 1622 the government began to lay restrictions on the cutting of timber, from an apprehension that a scarcity might ensue of proper materials for ship building.   But it was not till 1776 that, in consequence of a dispute between the then governor and the general of Marine, a Junta was appointed to superintend the woods, by whom various ordinances were published for their regulation.

In 1789 a decree was issued by which the royal right of felling was extended to all the woods of Cuba, of such trees as were suitable to naval purposes, and penalties were laid on the contravention of the decree.   The *Consulado* (or chamber of commerce) having represented the injury sustained by this infringement on the rights of property, measures were taken to soften the severity of the royal ordinance, but it was not till 1815 that effectual relief was given by the total abrogation of all foregoing restrictions and the renunciation of interference with private rights. By a decree dated 23rd June 1819, timber cut and used in the island is freed from all duties. Foreign timber pays 21½ per cent.

The eastern part of the island is most abounding in wood. It contains also some mines of copper which are not worked. *Lima* formerly supplied the island with copper of very inferior quality, for the use of the sugar engines, but England and the United States have superseded all other competitors and substituted iron for that use.

Fruit trees are found abundant in all parts of the island. Near the principal towns, the petty farmers on the *estancias* usually gain from six to eight dollars per annum, from each *coco* and *zapote* tree. The *mamey colorado* and the *narangero de china* (china orange) produce about three or four dollars per annum. The *plaintain* also liberally bestows its pleasant and nutritious produce, affording support and income to the poorest and most indolent. It bears but once, and the only care requisite is, when you pluck its ponderous bunches, to cut the stem which bore them and

H

in less than a month, a young progeny of suckers spring up in its place.

These latter plants (which, however, rise from five to eight feet high) are usually found round the huts as you proceed inland, and by their broad bright green leaves give a pleasing freshness to the scenery.

From Gibacoa to Matanzas the road lies over the mountains amidst woods and *potrero's*. There are, however, two other routes. One lies to the right of *Guanabacoa*, through the town of *Santa Maria del Rosario* to *Jaruco*. In this route one passes several lagoons in which a fish called *viegaca* is caught, small but of very fine flavour. In the various rivers, or rivulets, on the road, there are found eels, shrimps and fish called *guavina's ;* and on their banks tobacco is grown. The other route is also through *Jaruco*, breaking off from the *Gibacoa* road about half a league before you arrive at the first *ingenio*. This route leads through a crowded assemblage of *ingenio's* and caffetales. In the tract of country to the right are many ruined plantations *(ingenios demolidos)* or estates worked out of their fertility. A few leagues from *Jaruco* the country becomes mountainous; in one part nearly two miles in ascent, and the road so difficult that no carriages

can pass it. They are obliged to make a considerable circuit to arrive at *Jaruco*. This pass is very appropriately named *La loma de Cansavacas* (the hill for tiring cattle); the *Sierra*, on which it is situated, is called *La Escalera*, or the ladder.

San Juan de Jaruco is ten leagues from the Havana. It is a tolerably sized place having a *Cabildo*, but is not in any other respect worth notice. In the neighbourhood rice is cultivated to a small extent. The valley of *Los Guines*, S. W. of the Havana about twelve leagues, is the most favorable situation for the culture of rice. The country here is almost a perfect level through which the *Rio de los Guines* runs. Trenches are cut from the river for the purpose of irrigation. In times of drought they even water the fields with buckets. Several of the proprietors of *ingenios* have availed themselves of their local advantages and have erected water-mills on their estates. Towards the south coast, to which the *Rio de los Guines* runs, the land is so low that it is nothing but a swamp for some leagues and abounds with alligators. Most of the rivers on the S. coast have numbers of these formidable inhabitants. The people here, nay even the women, are said to be very dexterous in killing them.

To the west of the Havana lie many of the finest estates in the island, and the bays of *Honda*,

H 2

Santa Isabel and *la Guira*, with the port of *Mariel*, are not inferior to any in the whole range of coast. *Mariel* is seven leagues to the leeward or west of the *Havana*. It has only been opened as a free port, a few months, but bids fair to become a very flourishing place. Sir George Pocock, who commanded our fleet at the capture of the *Havana* in 1762, observes of this port, that " however trivial, with the possession of the " *Havana*, it may appear, yet I cannot help men- " tioning the discovery and possessing the har- " bour of *Mariel*, which we made ourselves " masters of, though the enemy had endeavoured " to ruin it by sinking ships in the entrance ; and " we had lately sent near one hundred sail of " transports, with some men of war there, for " security against the season." It was not easy to ruin a harbour which has twenty-two feet of water close in shore. Do not imagine I lend myself to the newspaper schemes of the English *Napoleonists,* when I observe, that if England had a port situated like *Mariel*, with the command of the gulfs of Mexico and Florida, the maritime security of her colonies would be perfected. Apropos, of Napoleonistic schemes ; it is not, I believe, generally known, that after the settlement of the French planters in *Cuba*, on their expulsion from *Santo Domingo*, a plan was formed by them and submitted to the government of France, for the cession of that part of the island lying to windward of a line to be drawn from *Baracoa*, (in 21° 4′ lat. N. and 76° 10′ long. W.) to *Trinidad*, which is in 21° 48′ 20″. lat. N. and 80° 0′ 52″ long. W. It is believed that the French government took steps to effectuate this measure, which were only frustrated by the course affairs took in Europe.*

* Joseph Buonaparte, the intrusive king of Spain, (better known to that nation by the title of *Pepe Batella*) sent one *Don Manuel Rodriguez Aleman y Pena* on a secret mission to this island in 1809. This individual arrived, from Norfolk, U. S at the Havana, on the 18th July in that year. Suspicion attaching to him, his effects were examined, and in the false bottom of a trunk, thirty-three letters were discovered. These were signed by Joseph Buonaparte, and directed to the principal persons here, at Mexico, Goatemala, Santa Fe, Merida de Yucatan, Caraccas and Puerto Rico. Don Manuel was adjudged guilty of treason, and executed at the Havana on the 30th of July.

LETTER VII.

Climate of Cuba. Sickly season. Rains. *Nortés,* or north
winds. Winter season. Table of the weather and thermo-
metrical range during twelve months. Produce of the
climate. Black cattle. Horses. Venomous creatures :
Snakes ; aranas peludas ; scorpions ; mosquito's. Birds.
Cocuyo, or fire-fly. Cuba blood-hound. Review of the
character of the people and resources of the island. The
abolition of the slave trade shown to be favourable to the real
and permanent interests of the island. Conclusion.

I HAVE not yet, I believe, given you an account of the climate of Cuba. Lying on the
northern verge of the tropic of Capricorn, it is,
in a great measure, exempted from those tremendous hurricanes which nearly shake to their
foundations the more southern islands. Earth-
quakes also are very rare. As to heat, it lies
within the tropics, and therefore, its extent may
be understood ; but, still, in these larger islands,
the height of their mountains and the quantity of
uncultivated surface they present, varies considerably the nature of their climate. For this reason

the same island has different degrees of temperature, and affords situations more or less adapted
to the European constitution.

I do not imagine there is a town in the West
Indies so replete with the seeds of mortality as
the *Havana.* Its low circumvallated situation ;
its fortifications ; the amount and nature of its
population ; their habits of living, and the range
of shore round its harbour, low and swampy,
unite in producing pestiferous effects. A league
inland to the eastward, there is a considerable rise
of ground, and, in that situation, the ravage of
fever is inconsiderable. Still further inland, on
the higher grounds, sufficiently clear to dissipate
damps, but not to deprive the soil of its fresh and
vital principle ; the inhabitants know no other
diseases than those which are the usual consequences of careless exposure, such as diarrhœas,
colds, &c. It is observed of these persons, that
they are equally liable to the yellow fever, with
the recently arrived European, on going to reside
in the Havana. Frequent instances, also, occur
of persons arriving at this city from the *Costa
firme* suffering from the malady.

The months of August and September are the
most unhealthy of the year ; the dry heated air is
greatly *disoxygenized* (if I may use the term) and
receives from the effluvia of this city many malig-

nant additions. The season of 1819 was unusually
hot and dry, and consequently, very sickly. The
average of the deaths in the *Havana*, during
August and September of that year, was *twenty-
five* per day.

About the middle of October the autumnal
rains are expected, which lower the temperature
considerably, and give rise to catarrhal and rheu-
matic disorders. The heaviest English rain is a
summer shower to the fall in the tropics. The
descent of water is so heavy, that, in a few
minutes, you will see the ravines and gullies,
which yawn on all sides, flowing with the force of
a cataract. On the first fall of rain after a
drought, the suffocating streams of caloric that
surround you give an idea of the heat with which
the soil is impregnated. In the dry season, the
bare rocky portion of it, which surrounds the
Havana, encreases the heat greatly, by reflecting
the rays of the sun ; but is highly advantageous
in the wet seasons by throwing off the water,
which, however, sinking into the vallies, may,
possibly, by the formation of marshes, more than
balance the first named benefit. But a judicious
observer might select many situations within a
league or two of the *Havana*, entirely free from
these inconveniences, where on a dry sheltered
eminence, the sultry south winds cannot waft in-

jurious *miasmata,* and the blasts from the north are sufficiently broken and tempered to come " with healing on their wings."

These latter winds begin to blow about November or December, rough, it is true, very frequently, but highly restorative to the decomposed elements of the atmosphere and the languid frame, exhausted by the long continuance of heat. To my English feelings they are peculiarly agreeable, possibly because I am not yet reduced to that porous relaxation which constitutes perfect *seasoning ;* but the *Cubano's* shrink at the sturdy blast, covering themselves round with their heavy *capotes* and binding handkerchiefs about their heads when they venture out. The labouring class, I can easily conceive, may be injured by the perspiratory check of the *nortès,* but the lounger, like myself, must surely be benefitted by the refrigerant air bath they afford.

December, January, February, and March, are the most agreeable months of the year. It is the period of the sugar harvest, the latter month of the maiz crop. In December the orange trees are covered with their beautiful fruit, ripe and delicious. The tamarind tree, also, in March, is loaded with its pendulous produce, so grateful and cooling. Vegetation is at its height. The most brilliant verdure covers the country, and the sky is usually clear and sparkling. This is the only one of the tropical seasons that should be painted dancing or with the air of divinity. The others are the daughters of *Baal,* delighting in the scorching blaze and human sacrifice.

The following summary of the state of the thermometer and weather for the last twelve months will be more satisfactory than my descriptive relation. It was made at *Guanabacoa,* four or five miles from the Havana, and as the thermometer (*fahrenheit*) hung in a room with a perpetual current passing through it (for I told you the windows are not glazed, but only open-barred) it gives a fair account of the temperature in the shaded air.

OCTOBER 1819.

During the first fortnight the thermometer averaged at six o'clock A. M. 77°. At twelve o'clock 82°. At nine P. M. 79°. During the last fortnight at six A. M. 74°. At twelve 79°. At nine P. M. 75°.—Greatest height observed 1st Oct. was 84° at mid-day. Lowest grade 73° at six A. M. Oct. 23d. Range 11°.

The commencement of the month sultry, with thunder. Rain every day for the last fortnight, nearly without intermission.

NOVEMBER.

The first part of the month, the thermometer

at six A. M. from 69° to 71°. At mid-day 75°. At nine P. M. 73°. The latter part of the month at six A. M. 69°. At mid-day 74°. At nine P. M. 71°. —Greatest height 78°; lowest, 67°. Range 11°.

Generally fair weather with rough blasts from N. E. towards the end.

DECEMBER.

During this month the thermometer has been usually 68° at six A. M. ; 73° at mid-day ; 70° at nine P. M. During the two or three days on which it rained the glass fell, at night, to 61°.— Greatest heighth 78°. Range 17°.

The temperature, and weather serene and agreeable.

JANUARY 1820.

Little variation in the thermometer from the course of last month.—Greatest height 78°; lowest grade 70°. Range 7°.

Cool, dry and serene during the whole month.

FEBRUARY.

The first part of this month the glass 72° in the morning; 76° at mid-day; 70° at night. About the middle of the month 80° at mid-day. The latter part of it was cooled by a fresh wind from N. E.—Greatest height 82°; lowest grade 69°. Range 13°.

Dry throughout with a sensibly increasing heat till the last week.

MARCH.

Thermometer nearly equal throughout. In the morning 76°; mid-day 81°; night 78°.—Highest grade 82°; lowest 73°. Range 9°.

Dry throughout with fresh winds from N. E.

APRIL.

In the morning 74°; mid-day 79°; night 75°, with trifling variation during the whole of the month. Only three days of rain, but this and the encreasing gales from the N. E. freshened the air greatly.—Greatest height 81°; lowest grade 71°. Range 11°.

MAY.

Nearly the same temperature as last month for the first fortnight, the glass being seldom higher than 80°. The latter part of the month it suddenly became sultry; the glass 79° in the morning; 84° at mid-day; 81° at night.—Highest grade 86°; lowest 75°. Range 11°.

A few showers at the beginning. South winds and thunder towards the end.

JUNE.

In the morning the glass usually 78°; at mid-day 81°; at night 79°.—Highest grade 85°; lowest 78°. Range 7°.

Rain nearly every day.

JULY.

Very equal throughout; 79° in the morning;

85° at mid-day ; 80° at night.—Highest grade 87° ;
lowest 79°. Range 8°.

A few showers occasionally and heavy thunder.
During the two last months the days have been
refreshed by the sea breeze, which sets in about
ten in the morning, and lasts till five in the after-
noon. The evenings rather sultry and mosquitoes
numerous.

AUGUST.

Little difference from the course of last month.
Towards the middle, the glass at 88° at two o'clock
P. M. On the 30th a heavy storm of wind and
rain came on from the s. w. The glass fell to 78°,
but rose again on the succeeding day to 84°.
Range 10°.

SEPTEMBER.

This month set in temperate with some rain.
Thermometer—morning 78°; noon 84 ; night
80°.—It advanced rather after the first week, but
on the whole the average height was 85°; lowest
grade 77°. Range 8°.

The annual range of the thermometer observed
in a course of years has been nearly *fifty* degrees,
for in some winters the temperature has been near
the freezing point and in some summers about 92
degrees.

From this account of the climate you may infer

the nature of the productions of the island. Sugar, coffee, and tobacco have become its staples to the exclusion of almost every other species of cultivation. Cotton is absolutely neglected. A small portion of indigo only is produced. Pimento and ginger are not thought of. Cochineal has not been attempted, though there is sufficiency of the *nopal*, or, as it is here called, *tuna*.

The black cattle are a very fine breed and are used in great numbers to draw produce. Sheep are rare, a few only being kept, rather as curiosities than as stock. The hogs are most abundant, and form the favorite meat of the lower orders, most of whom keep them. Horses and mules are bred in the island but a great many of the latter are imported from the *Costa firme*, and of the former, a large bony breed called *frisones* (or *frieslanders*) are brought from North America. These are not found to thrive, the first hot summer carrying them off. The price of horses ranges from sixty to five hundred dollars ; the usual price of a decent serviceable horse being two hundred dollars.

Venomous creatures this island is, happily, almost entirely free from. The snakes found here are very similar to those that infest the woods in England, and are very shy of society. Their bite is not mortal. The worst of the venomous spe-

cies is the *arana peluda*, or hairy spider, a hideous
reptile, as large as a man's hand, covered with
brown hair. The bite is considered highly dangerous. The scorpion is so common that its frequency almost takes off the feeling of the dread
with which it would otherwise be regarded. It
is, when fully grown, as large as the *arana peluda*,
with a long jointed tail which it carries curved
over its back, but is extended at pleasure. The
sting is at the end. The effect (for I speak from
experience) is sharp and painful and creates a
local paralysis, but wears off through time and
the application of spirits. The *mosquito* must,
though insignificant, be ranked in this order, for its
sting, to the recently imported, is frequently very
troublesome and productive of much pain and
eruption.

Amongst the wants of the country and which
an English ear, attuned to the melody of its native
groves, almost directly discovers, is the total absence of birds of song.

But if the evening hour is deprived of the notes
of the nightingale, it is enriched by the brightness
of the *cocuyo*, or *fire-fly*. This singular insect bears
in the upper parts of its head a phosphoric light,
like that of the glow-worm and numbers are seen
circling in the air like meteors. It is perfectly
harmless and too often suffers from peurile tyranny
on this account.

Amongst the animal rarities of the island let me
not forget to notice the *Cuba blood-hound*, that
celebrated friend of the whites and enemy of the
blacks.   In chief and general air he is not much
unlike the English mastiff, but possesses all the
ferocity of the bull-dog.   Every plantation has
several of these creatures for the pursuit of *cimar-
rones*, or fugitive negroes, and the preservation of
the whites, as the negroes stand in more dread of
one of these ferocious brutes than of an armed over-
seer.   I have no reason, however, to believe that
they are employed otherwise than as *guides* in the
pursuit of fugitives and house-guards for their
masters; but it is undoubted that the spirit of
persecution against the unhappy negroes is instill-
ed and fostered by every kind of encouragement
and allurement, for I deny that nature (as some
allege) has violated her own feelings and principles by making the blood-hound a natural enemy
to the man of colour.   In England you have often
noticed the sagacity with which a pampered
house-dog scents out and attacks a beggar, who
has fewer distinctive marks than the slave.   The
principle of education is the same, and insolent
tyranny of persecution equally the effect of human
instruction.

I cannot enter into a minuter detail of the
animal and vegetable peculiarities of the island,
nor do I think it necessary; for the productions

of both classes are nearly the same as in the other islands which are well known to the English. I have glanced at all that came within my range of vision and detailed to you what my eye perceived, without attempting a philosophical research. My object has been to acquire a knowledge of the character of the people and of the resources of the island, more for the purposes of the business of life than of closet speculation. Probably (as you and I usually see things in the same light) you will agree with me on the results of my observation.

The people of Cuba appear to me to have a more local and segregate character and to be less firmly tied to the mother country, than the inhabitants of any other West India island. The opinion is pretty openly expressed by many that, though the root is in Europe, the flower blows here and contains seeds sufficient for raising an entire plant in the same soil. When these political botanists are acquainted with geography and statistics they will undoubtedly be wiser.

The native of every country thinks his own the first region in the universe, but the Spaniard goes farther, he considers *himself* the centre of his circle. As every house is a palace where a king resides, so every spot, on which a *Spaniard* has settled, becomes dignified, for his pure Gothic

I

blood is kept flowing from this new fountain and
the *halo* of his glory rests on the soil. Thus the
American Spaniards brought from the Peninsula
what constituted its fame—*themselves ;* centuries
of residence have identified them with the countries they conquered, and the name of a *colonist*
they consider as a stigma. From these causes
they regard their domiciles in this quarter of the
globe by no means as of secondary consequence.
The constitution recognizes *all* the Spanish dominions as equal, though the delegation of deputies
to the present cortes has not been made on this
principle.

Perhaps notions of this nature may influence
people here, and the pride of individuals is not
checked by public considerations. They wish to
dignify the country *they* live in—it is their *own*
and, consequently, in every way worthy. It is popular logic and, added to considerations far more
weighty and argumentative, has separated more
than half the S. American provinces from the
Spanish dominion.

In no community can questions of public interest more warmly affect than here. No sooner
is a point of this nature thrown upon the opinions
of the people, than with chemical effect, you see
them divided and discomposed into turbid portions. A strong effervescence takes place for the

moment, but the sperme and noise soon subside
and a ferocious crowd, that a little before were
ready to tear a fellow creature to pieces, sink into
apathy, as if to regain strength for a new burst.
Notwithstanding all this collective fury, *public
spirit* is wanting, that soul of social enterprize
without which a nation is only a mass of strangers
and sojourners. · Whatever is done here by the
people *as a public*, will proceed from the concurrence of private interests which may embody
individuals. Each acting from attention to his
own views, it may sometimes happen that many
will accord in the promotion of a measure, and
they will support it the more warmly because
allied to their private interests.

The freedom of commerce enjoyed by the
island for the last eleven years has very much
tended to *nationalize* the *Cubano's*. They know
it is a grant forced from the mother country and
they have full evidence how little it is in her
power to aid their commercial wants. Of nearly
twelve hundred vessels which annually enter the
port of Havana, eight hundred are foreign.
They are thus made acquainted with their own
importance.

The number of white established inhabitants,
and the luxury of a large city, are circumstances
more favourable than the other islands possess.

I 2

The exporting vessels are drawn hither with import cargoes, and the benefit of the latter tends
to lower the freight of export.   As Mexico still
labours under restriction from foreign commerce,
there is a considerable re-export from the Havana
to *Vera Cruz*, *Sisal* and *Campeachy*.   Goods to
the value of nearly three millions are thus re-
shipped in Spanish bottoms, and produce to the
same amount exported by the foreign vessels that
brought them.   It is not to be expected that
Mexico will long remain in a state of exclusion,
and therefore the island will suffer this diminution
of her trade.   It is not to be doubted also, but
that the abolition of the slave trade will have the
effect of checking the augmentation of produce.
There is a certain point beyond which the amount
of the present staples could not have risen ;
because the requisition of them by European or
American consumers would not always be on the
increase, nor would the ratio of imports be likely
to keep the alluring proportion they now bear to
the exports.   But this point has not yet been
approximated, for, though the mass of native
whites are poor and indolent, yet enterprizing
speculators would have, probably, settled here as
planters, as very many have done during the last
twenty years.   Notwithstanding, I am inclined
to think the island will be considerably benefitted

by the abolition. The island of Cuba is entitled
to rank higher than a mere sugar colony. The
variety and richness of its soil render it fully
capable of other field products within the ability
of *white* cultivators. The vast tracts of country
yet untouched or unoccupied, if divided into
small farms or *estancia's* amongst white settlers,
either native or foreign, would encrease the
wealth and population of the island in a higher
degree than if its surface was covered with sugar
and coffee.

This course will, probably, be followed since
the impossibility (it is hoped) of acquiring new
negroes from Africa, will oblige capitalists to invest their money in other ways than in plantations which can only be cultivated by them. By
purchasing large tracts of lands, and sub-letting
them to the industrious at equitable rents ; en-
couraging the production of articles of subsistence,
of lumber, &c. for the supply of the other islands ;
establishing manufactories of various kinds, suitable to the country, and the wants of the South
American markets, to which they will have the
most favoured access ; or, by rendering the
island a depot for Europe and the north ;—by
these means the island would be most essentially
benefitted, and become a worthy neighbour of the
United States, which have risen in the course of

one hundred and fifty years from colonies and plantations, to be one of the first nations of the world.

Previous to opening the ports of the island to a free trade, this seems to have been the course speculation was taking. In the years 1806, 1807, and 1808, sales of land to the value of 11,548 dollars were made. In 1809 (the year in which the ports were opened) not a single *caballeria* was sold by the government. In the subsequent year (1810) only 385 dollars were recieved for the purchase of land. As the abolition of the *slave trade* is in fact shutting up the ports of the island against a great traffic, and forms a con-sequential restriction upon the exports of the articles raised by the labour of negroes, the prin-ciple of both is the same, and from the examples adduced, we may anticipate the like result.

There can be no doubt that the happiness of the future generations of *Cubano's* will be advanced by the present abolition. *Santo Domingo* lies full in the sight of this island. Its terrific past history and frowning future, one would think must sufficiently impress its neighbour with the policy and necessity of solely augmenting its white population. I can vouch for their ability to labour in this climate. The great obstacle to *white* exertion is the *slavery of the blacks,* which gives a debased character to manual exertion. As the examples of this are reduced, the number of white labourers will be augmented.

A wise and vigorous government would, I am convinced, in the space of half a century, render the island of Cuba stable and orderly in its social arrangement, active and numerous as to population, and as replete with resources, both for public and private purposes, as any territory of its extent. That it may attain this heigth of character, and the graves of its aboriginial possessors be covered with atoning monuments, raised by the superior worth of the descendants of their destroyers, is what no one can desire more earnestly than I do.

FINIS.

Printed by W. Molineux, Bream's Buildings, Chancery Lane.

For EU product safety concerns, contact us at Calle de José Abascal, 56–1°, 28003 Madrid, Spain or eugpsr@cambridge.org.

www.ingramcontent.com/pod-product-compliance
Ingram Content Group UK Ltd.
Pitfield, Milton Keynes, MK11 3LW, UK
UKHW012339130625
459647UK00009B/398